Generic Pipelines Using Docker

The DevOps Guide to Building Reusable, Platform Agnostic CI/CD Frameworks

Brandon Atkinson
Dallas Edwards

Apress®

Generic Pipelines Using Docker

Brandon Atkinson
North Chesterfield, VA, USA

Dallas Edwards
Midlothian, VA, USA

ISBN-13 (pbk): 978-1-4842-3654-3
https://doi.org/10.1007/978-1-4842-3655-0

ISBN-13 (electronic): 978-1-4842-3655-0

Library of Congress Control Number: 2018962365

Managing Director, Apress Media LLC: Welmoed Spahr
Acquisitions Editor: Joan Murray
Development Editor: Laura Berendson
Coordinating Editor: Jill Balzano

Cover image designed by Freepik (www.freepik.com)

Distributed to the book trade worldwide by Springer Science+Business Media New York, 233 Spring Street, 6th Floor, New York, NY 10013. Phone 1-800-SPRINGER, fax (201) 348-4505, e-mail orders-ny@springer-sbm.com, or visit www.springeronline.com. Apress Media, LLC is a California LLC and the sole member (owner) is Springer Science + Business Media Finance Inc (SSBM Finance Inc). SSBM Finance Inc is a **Delaware** corporation.

For information on translations, please e-mail rights@apress.com, or visit www.apress.com/rights-permissions.

Apress titles may be purchased in bulk for academic, corporate, or promotional use. eBook versions and licenses are also available for most titles. For more information, reference our Print and eBook Bulk Sales web page at www.apress.com/bulk-sales.

Any source code or other supplementary material referenced by the author in this book is available to readers on GitHub via the book's product page, located at www.apress.com/9781484236543. For more detailed information, please visit www.apress.com/source-code.

Printed on acid-free paper

Table of Contents

About the Authors

Brandon Atkinson is a software engineer with more than 14 years of industry experience encompassing analysis, design, development, and implementation of enterprise-level solutions. His passion is building scalable teams and enterprise architecture that can transform businesses and alleviate pain points. He has extensive experience in various technologies/methodologies, including Azure, AWS, .NET, DevOps, Cloud, JavaScript, Angular, Node.js, and more. Brandon lives in Richmond, Virginia, USA with his wife and two daughters.

Dallas Edwards has more than ten years of experience as a software engineer. He thrives on creating solutions that are pragmatic, scale easily, and that are easy to test and maintain. His experience encompasses a wide range of expertise, including software development, iOS application development, and DevOps. Dallas lives in Richmond, Virginia, USA with his wife and is an avid scuba diver.

About the Technical Reviewer

 **Alex Fabian** is a professional software engineer with experience building enterprise-scale Java systems, APIs, and web applications. He has hands-on experience implementing Docker-based deployment pipelines for microservices and has spent considerable time integrating with various offerings from Amazon Web Services. Alex has had the opportunity to work on large- *and* small-scale projects for Fortune 500 companies, technology startups, government contractors, and small organizations. He holds certifications from Amazon Web Services and a B.S. in Computer Science from The University of Virginia.

Acknowledgments

Brandon Atkinson

Writing a book is very hard work, and very time consuming. I could not have done this without the support of my family, especially my amazing wife Jennie and my wonderful kids. I also want to thank Dallas for coming on this journey with me. I did my best to take over your life; you're about to get it back! I also want to thank Chris Bowers for setting me on this DevOps path, and providing a lot of the vision that made this pattern come true.

Dallas Edwards

There's no way this could've happened without the constant support and encouragement of my family. I am so grateful for the role each of you has played in my life.

I'd like to thank Brandon for giving me this opportunity. I can't wait to see what you drag me into next!

Finally, to my wife Cierra: thank you so much for all of your advice and sticking with me through all the late nights. I already proved it.

Introduction

DevOps (a clipped compound of "development" and "operations") is a software engineering culture and practice that aims at unifying software development (Dev) and software operation (Ops). The main characteristic of the DevOps movement is to strongly advocate automation and monitoring at all steps of software construction, from integration, testing, and releasing to deployment and infrastructure management.

That definition pretty much sums up what most people think of when they hear the term DevOps. Not because it perfectly describes what it is, however; it leaves you more confused than before you asked the question "What is DevOps?". DevOps comes in so many forms it can be hard to nail down exactly what it is. I've worked in a lot of different shops in my time and DevOps is always something different at each stop.

For most it involves developers writing code that is checked into source control, which immediately kicks off a build pipeline that deploys your application. That pipeline will perform various steps that may include stages like building, testing, and deploying. From my experience, if you're just doing these simple steps through automation, you're way ahead of some. However, for many this is not enough to have your organization be considered as fully embracing DevOps.

You may also want to include things like automated infrastructure creation, security scans, static code analysis, and more. In an ideal situation everything you do in a software shop is stored as code in source control. This includes your application code, infrastructure scripts, database scripts, networking setup, etc. With a push of a button everything your application needs to run can be created on the fly. For a lot shops, this is what it means to truly embrace DevOps.

Some organizations are more mature than others when it comes to DevOps practices. In my experience you're well on your way to maturity if you're doing the following items:

- You deploy your application via an automated pipeline.

- Once built and tested, application code binaries can be promoted via an automated pipeline.

I realize a lot of people will look at that list and exclaim "WHAT?!". There are only two items, and your organization may be way beyond those. However, most are not and would see immense improvements by just doing these two things. If you're one of the folks who thinks this list is crazy small, then count yourself lucky. I know many people who would kill for just these two items.

Automated pipelines in my opinion are the lifeblood of good DevOps practices. They provide so many benefits to both the team of developers as well as the business that relies on their code. A well-crafted pipeline gives you a repeatable process for building, testing, and deploying your application. It can be used to create artifacts that, once built, are simply promoted, ensuring that what makes it to Production has been tested and vetted.

Pipelines can also be a pain point for organizations as well. You may have multiple applications, each written in different languages, and each with their own finicky way of being built. It can be a nightmare at times jumping between technologies, debugging the various stages, and keeping the lights on. Luckily modern technology is helping us get around some of these issues. Technology like Docker has given us an opportunity to standardize our platforms. By utilizing Docker in your pipeline, you can give your developers some peace of mind that if they can build it, so can you.

Combine this with cloud technology like Amazon ECS or Azure Container Service and now we can extend that piece of mind all the way to deployment. If it runs locally in your Docker daemon, it will run in the cloud. This even applies if you're running an enterprise cloud platform like Nutanix or Dell; if the destination is a container orchestration service you're golden. Now, consider that .NET Core is open source and can run on Linux, and you've pretty much covered all your bases. It's a great time to be in technology!

This book aims to show how you can use all this technology to simplify your pipelines and make them truly generic. Imagine a single pipeline that deploys all your code regardless of the tech stack it is written in. It's not a dream; we'll show you how.

Who This Book is For

This book was written with the DevOps professional in mind who may be struggling with writing and maintaining multiple pipelines. However, it's also for anyone in technology who is interested in learning about building generic pipelines.

You don't have to be a DevOps master to get a lot from this book; however, you will benefit more with experience in the following areas:

- *Docker*: Being familiar with Docker from creating Dockerfiles, building and running images, etc. We won't get very deep into Docker, but a working knowledge is key.

- *Bash Scripts*: Most of the examples in this book are written in Bash. You should have at least some minimal experience with scripts.

- *CI/CD Platform Experience*: You'll be much better off if you already have experience with a platform like Circle CI or Jenkins. However, throughout the book we'll walk you through working with these platforms.

As you can see, having some DevOps and pipeline experience will certainly benefit you as you read this book, but it's not a hard requirement. If you're a developer of any type, you should have no issues jumping right into the examples in this book. As stated, the future of DevOps and pipelines is everything is code. If you're comfortable writing code, you'll be fine.

Why We Wrote This Book

This book is the culmination of a lot of hard work our team has done over the last year. We were tasked with creating a generic, reusable pipeline that any development team could utilize regardless of the language they were writing in. Our organization was going through a transformation from monolithic applications to microservices, and the old way of delivering code wasn't going to cut it.

After we decided on our plan of attack and began implementing, we realized we had something special on our hands. Talking with other groups around us, no one was tackling CI/CD pipelines in quite the same way. Most were still building a pipeline per application. Some were taking a step further and building tech stack–specific pipelines that could work with teams using the same language. However, no one was going the extra step and building a single pipeline for all.

Now that we've been iterating on our code for a while we've seen some amazing results. Our development teams can quickly produce microservices and on-board them to the pipeline in a matter of minutes. By utilizing Docker locally on the developer's machines and in the pipeline, we can ensure that the experience is extremely similar. Using Docker in the pipeline gives us full control over the process regardless of what the underlying platform has installed.

We've seen this pattern take hold in our group and how it's transformed the way we deliver code. This book is our effort to share what we've learned and hopefully pass along some of that knowledge. If you come away from this book with even a few things you find useful, we'll take that as a success. If you end up taking this pattern and applying it in your organization—even better. We've seen its successes and believe in it 100%!

What We Won't Cover in This Book

This book is meant to show you how to build generic pipelines utilizing Docker. We won't be covering any CI/CD principles (except by reference), or talking about the benefits of DevOps and how it can transform your organization. We're going to assume you are either already on-board with these concepts or at least know about them in some way.

There are many well-written books out there that extoll the benefits of proper continuous integration and delivery. We don't need to hash all that out here, nor could we do a better job than those before us. We won't be covering Agile principles or how to write better software. We won't argue which CI/CD platform is better or which language produces the best code.

While you're in this book we're going to focus on why monolithic applications and their pipelines are bad. How microservices and smaller pipelines are good. We'll follow that up with why generic reusable pipelines are even better. Then we'll wrap all that up with a lot of examples. So, if you want or need a deep dive into the benefits of DevOps and proper CI/CD practices, search out another book. If you want to build leaner more efficient pipelines, read on.

What You'll Need

Before moving on we'll need to cover the items you'll need to work with the examples in this book. The first few chapters deal with why you want to look at generic pipelines, and later chapters present implementing an example. So, you will not immediately need all of these. If you like, you can read ahead and deal with these later. If you prefer to be prepared ahead of time, here is what you'll need:

- Mac or Windows 10

- Docker for Mac/Windows

- IntelliJ IDEA (or another IDE)

- CI/CD Platform

- Docker Hub Account

- GitHub Account

Let's dig into each of these and walk through installing, signing up, and configuring each.

Mac or Windows 10

At first glance you may be thinking "Why include a section on this? Of course we have one of these." You would not be entirely wrong for thinking this, but there is a good reason. If you're on a Mac you're all set, you are set up well for what's about to come. If you're on a Windows machine, we need to talk.

We highly recommend using Windows 10 if your only option is Windows. The main reason for this is the Docker experience. In Windows 10, Docker is a first-class citizen and the experience closely matches that on a Mac. In addition, Windows 10 now supports the Linux subsystem, which allows you to use Bash natively.

We also realize not everyone can be on the latest hardware and operating systems. You should be able to complete all the examples in this book with any operating system that you can install Docker on. However, this means you may have to jump through more hoops to get everything working correctly. As we move forward, we will assume you are either on a Mac or Windows 10.

Caution   Realistically, Windows 7 is about as low as you can go with an earlier Windows release. While it is possible to install Docker on Windows 7, some of the other items we'll use in this book, like Bash, will be outside your reach natively on that platform. You can still utilize them; it will just need to be within the context of a Docker container or virtual machine.

Docker for Mac/Windows

It goes without saying that you'll need Docker for this book—it's in the title! Luckily Docker provides a free Community Edition for both Mac and Windows 10 users. Navigate to `www.docker.com/docker-mac` or `www.docker.com/docker-windows` as shown in Figure I-1.

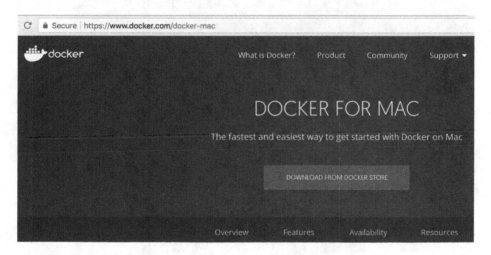

Figure I-1. *Download page from docker.com*

Click the "Download from Docker Store" button to be taken to the official Docker Store download page as shown in Figure I-2.

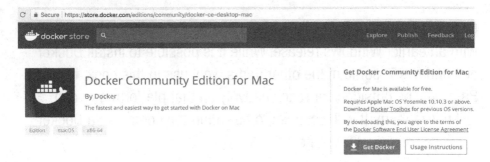

Figure I-2. *Docker Community Edition download page for Mac. The Windows download page is almost identical.*

Click the "Get Docker" link to download Docker. Follow the instructions to install Docker on your machine. Once installed, you will see the Docker icon in the top left of your screen as shown in Figure I-3. Clicking the icon will open the menu.

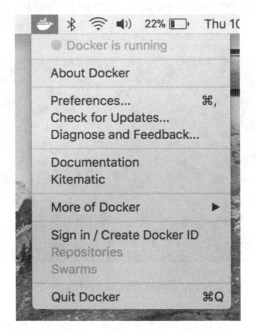

Figure I-3. *Docker icon and menu after a successful installation*

On Windows 10 the icon will appear in the bottom right tray. You can also verify the installation by running a **docker -v** command in the terminal, as shown in Figure I-4. If you're on Windows you can run this command from PowerShell.

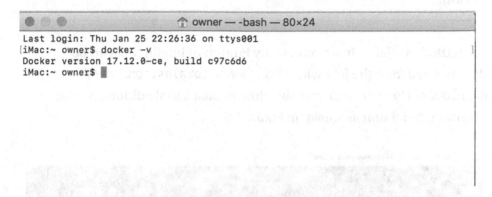

```
● ● ●                    🏠 owner — -bash — 80×24
Last login: Thu Jan 25 22:26:36 on ttys001
[iMac:~ owner$ docker -v
Docker version 17.12.0-ce, build c97c6d6
iMac:~ owner$ █
```

Figure I-4. *Verifying your Docker installation via the terminal*

Note   When downloading Docker, make note of the supported versions for your operating system. As of this writing, Mac OS Yosemite 10.10.3 or above and Windows 10 Professional or Enterprise 64-bit are supported. If you are using an earlier release of your OS, you can opt to install Docker Toolbox (https://docs.docker.com/toolbox/overview/). However, please be aware that Toolbox is not a full-fledged Docker experience.

IntelliJ IDEA

In this book we'll be using JetBrains IntelliJ IDEA as our IDE of choice. However, any IDE can be used and if you have one already installed and are comfortable with it, feel to use that. If you want to use IntelliJ, then continue reading; otherwise jump to the next section.

Note Any screenshots taken of an IDE in this book will be of IntelliJ on Mac. However, there is nothing stopping you from using a different IDE. All code examples will work the same regardless of what you are using.

JetBrains offers a free Community Edition of IntelliJ that can be downloaded from the following URL: www.jetbrains.com/idea/download/. There are two available downloads: a trial edition and the Community Edition as shown in Figure I-5.

Figure I-5. *IntelliJ download page on the JetBrains website*

The Community Edition has more than enough features to get you through this book and beyond. Download this edition, and follow the normal installation. Once installed and launched, you'll be greeted with the "Welcome to IntelliJ IDEA" screen as shown in Figure I-6. If you see this screen, your install was successful and you can move on to the next section.

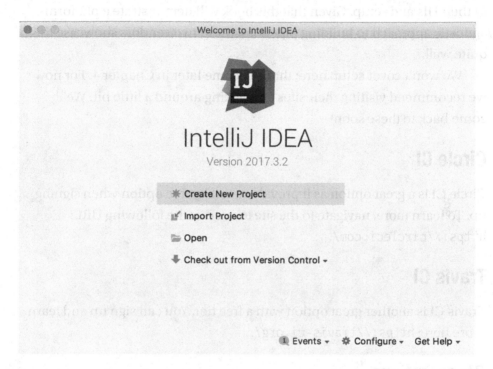

Figure I-6. The welcome screen upon launching IntelliJ for the first time

CI/CD Platform

To showcase how you can build platform agnostic pipelines, we'll need some platforms to work with. We'll work with two of the more popular platforms on the market: Circle CI and Travis CI. Outside of being popular options for building pipelines, they also provide free subscriptions via Software as a Service (SaaS) offerings. This was important so you could work through the examples without spending any money. Also, being SaaS, you don't need to worry about downloading and installing software, which is extremely nice!

Another reason we chose these two platforms is how different they are in their UIs and setup. Given that this book will demonstrate a platform agnostic approach to building pipelines, these two vendors showcase this quite well.

We won't cover setup here; that will come later in Chapter 4. For now we recommend visiting their sites and poking around a little bit. We'll come back to these soon!

Circle CI

Circle CI is a great option as it provides a totally free option when signing up. To learn more, navigate to the site located at the following URL: `https://circleci.com/`.

Travis CI

Travis CI is another great option with a free tier. You can sign up and learn more here: `https://travis-ci.org/`.

Other Options

If you've been working in DevOps for a while, you know there are many platforms out there to choose from. If you're new to DevOps, have no fear. If you don't like an offering from a vendor, you'll have plenty of options to find something different.

What we present in this book will work with any platform that offers running commands inside a Docker container. If you don't care for the platforms we're using in this book, there is nothing stopping you from using something different. These vendors were chosen because they offer a great product at a great price: Free! Also, these options are completely managed with SaaS solutions. This frees you up from having to deal with installations. However, if you like, here are some other options you can also use:

- JetBrains Teamcity TestDrive (`www.jetbrains.com/teamcity/`): JetBrains offers a 60-day trial of Teamcity TestDrive in the cloud. However, TestDrive is meant to be a trial in the web, and not meant for long-term use. At the end of the trail you are expected to download the product if you like it.

- CloudBees Jenkins (`www.cloudbees.com/`): Jenkins is a powerhouse in the DevOps world, so we'd be remiss to leave them out of this book. CloudBees offers a seven-day trial of their Enterprise product, which is hosted. There are some drawbacks. You need a company-provided email address to sign up, and did I mention the seven days?

Docker Hub Account

You'll also need an account on Docker Hub. In the examples you'll be building custom Docker images to perform your build and unit test stages in, so we'll need somewhere to store those. Docker provides free accounts on Docker Hub. To get started, navigate to `https://hub.docker.com/` as shown in Figure I-7.

Figure I-7. *Docker Hub landing page*

Fill out the form on the landing page and click the "Sign Up" page and you'll be all set. Once you're logged in you can create new repositories via the "Create Repository" button, as shown in Figure I-8. You'll need to create a new repository before pushing any images to Hub.

Figure I-8. *Docker Hub page after you've logged in*

GitHub Account

Finally, you'll need a GitHub account. As you noticed in the signup for Circle CI and VSTS, you'll eventually be connecting a GitHub account to them. To create an account, navigate to https://github.com/ and fill in the form located on the homepage, as seen in Figure I-9.

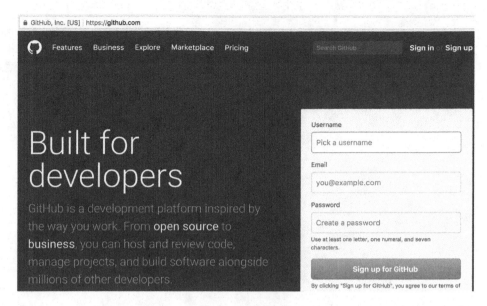

Figure I-9. *Sign up form on the GitHub landing page*

Once you sign up, you'll be taken to the main landing page where you can create new projects. For now you don't need to do anything else; you're all setup for the examples to come.

Overview

This introduction has gotten you prepared for the code examples that come later in the book. You should now have all the software installed and have created all the accounts needed. While actual coding and deployments come later in the book, I would encourage you to poke around and explore Circle CI and VSTS ahead of time. There are a lot of options available in each, and it would be good to build even a simple "Hello World" deployment before jumping into examples.

Next, we'll begin to look at how traditional monolithic applications and pipelines are holding you back. We'll explore why these came to be and how toxic they are for rapid delivery of applications.

CHAPTER 1

Recognizing You Are Stuck in the Past

It can seem sometimes that the world has lost its mind. You're plugging away writing code, building new features for your business users, and deploying code like a pro without a care in the world. Then along comes a new pattern or a blogger talking about new ways to write software and efficient means to deploy code. They talk about how they've observed that the way your organization does things is just plain wrong, if not barbaric. You might take it personally or get offended, and rightly so! Who are they to tell you that what you're doing is wrong; "we've always done it this way."

Recognizing you are stuck in the past can be difficult. Some of us refuse to acknowledge it or are comfortable in our ways of doing things, while others of us use it as an excuse to get upset or vent frustration about a project or the software we're building. Oftentimes, especially when you work for a larger company, you have no control over the situation you're in. I've worked for companies that have had feature requests pile up, which prevented any discussions of refactoring an application. When the business needs new features to bring in more money from demanding clients, it's tough to argue any other way.

In this chapter we'll look at how some organizations are truly stuck in the past. We'll explore why applications tend to evolve this way, or are born that way. We'll also discuss how these applications can lead to stress and

© Brandon Atkinson, Dallas Edwards 2018
B. Atkinson and D. Edwards, *Generic Pipelines Using Docker*,
https://doi.org/10.1007/978-1-4842-3655-0_1

discontent among teams, and some simple things you can do to mitigate stress and improve morale. This is not meant to be doom and gloom, but rather to help bring to light that things can be better.

Monolithic Applications

Monolith—something having a uniform, massive, redoubtable, or inflexible quality or character. ("monolith". Dictionary.com Unabridged. Random House, Inc. Jan 30, 2018. <Dictionary.com `www.dictionary.com/browse/monolith`>)

I think this sums up quite nicely some of the monolithic applications I have worked on in the past. Massive and inflexible are great ways to describe these applications. If you're not a software developer by trade and have never worked on an application like this, count yourself lucky. Those of us who have understand these definitions and how accurate they are. A traditional monolithic application looks like the design as shown in Figure 1-1.

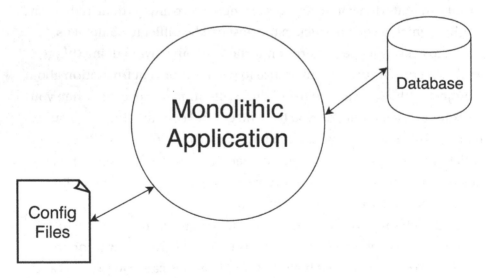

Figure 1-1. *Traditional monolithic application design*

Info   The word redoubtable is fitting as well, defined as "that is to be feared; formidable." ("redoubtable". Dictionary.com Unabridged. Random House, Inc. Jan 30, 2018. <Dictionary.com `www.dictionary.com/browse/redoubtable`>)

Here we have a huge application that connects to a database and has multiple configurations as it moves through various deployment environments. Sometimes the configuration isn't even separate, it's baked into the source code. In this scenario the user interface (UI) lives with, and is usually packaged with, the application code. Applications like this are usually built on MVC frameworks that bring front-end rendering and server-side code all in one neat package. These frameworks are great for rapid application development, but usually result in poor decisions in code structure, separation of concerns, and flow.

Some teams will logically make the next jump to an architecture that breaks the UI away from server-side code, much like the design shown in Figure 1-2.

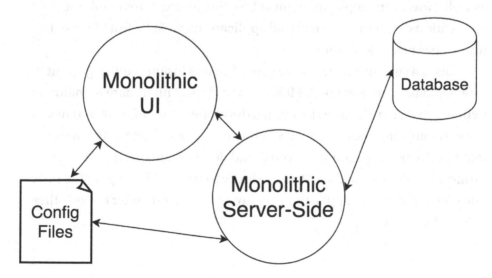

Figure 1-2. *Monolith that has been split into two layers*

While this is certainly a step in the right direction, it can introduce much more complexity. You've now effectively doubled up your deployment concerns. Even though the UI and server-side code are split from each other, they cannot be deployed independently. You'll now have two deployments of large code bases that must be coordinated. You may also now need to juggle configuration files: one for the UI and one for the server-side code.

In an ideal world you're deploying the application into multiple environments that may include: Development, QA, UAT, Staging, and Production. At each stage the configuration must change to point to the correct database. Also, presumably the database must be updated with any data or schema changes to support the code. In almost all scenarios changes in the application code or database are tightly coupled. So, a change in either concern forces a complete deployment of all the concerns. This is a lot of work if all you need to do is add a link to a page!

Now imagine if you have two or three of these applications. The deployment process becomes so much more complicated. It would not be unheard of that these applications have dependencies on each other as well. Now every deployment must be coordinated across multiple applications, or at the very least, all applications must be tested even if only one is being deployed.

This is a sure-fire way to drive your IT teams insane. Nothing about this process makes you feel good. Monoliths become a nightmare to maintain, debug, or add new features to. From a developer point of view, you never want to touch the code, especially in business-critical areas. As a system team (DevOps or Sys Admins), you dread deployments, as they are error prone and take a lot of time. If you're lucky to have a CI/CD pipeline in place to support your application, it may not be much better on the other side of the fence.

One Pipeline per Application

A lot of monolithic applications are still deployed manually, even in 2018! I've worked with several clients who had a system team that consisted of DBAs and Sys Admins. This was the de facto DevOps team, as they were responsible for deploying application code. The deployment process involved the developers manually building and packaging the code, and placing it on a shared drive or FTP folder on the network. A Sys Admin would then copy the compiled code and paste it on the production servers.

You might be reading this and thinking to yourself there is no way this is still going on. How can organizations deploy applications like this? Well, these practices exist for many of the same reasons as monoliths. Here's the short list:

- We've always done it this way.

- The deployment can't be automated.

- The business won't give us time to build it out.

- We don't have DevOps expertise.

The list can go on and on, and some of these may be valid; however, most simply reflect fear of doing something new or moving away from a method that works. If they are valid, they most likely need to be addressed and overcome. If your monolith is a commercial off-the-shelf product, you may not be able to automate the deployment. The business may have other very real and critical needs that need immediate attention. You may not want to take on building a pipeline if you don't have the expertise, or the time to dedicate to it.

Note   Commercial off-the-shelf (COTS) applications can pose a real challenge. While there are many well-written and maintained COTS products, some are a real nightmare. A quality COTS application can be easily deployed via a pipeline. Others require custom deployment processes that make using a pipeline nearly impossible.

If you're lucky enough to have a pipeline for your monolith, it can at times add to your headaches. In almost all scenarios, you will build one that is tightly coupled to your application. In fact, this practice has nothing to do with monoliths per se. Most CI/CD pipelines and processes are built around a single application. They are custom built to do everything needed by the application and can include things like:

- Building the application

- Automated tests

- Running security or static code analysis

- Provisioning/configuring infrastructure

- Publishing artifacts

- Injecting configuration

- Deploying the application

These pipelines do everything they should to get the application where it needs to go, and the state it needs to be in. You may even be able to reuse some sections of the pipeline elsewhere, like security or static code scans. However, in most cases the pipeline is very coupled to the specific needs of the application being deployed. For instance, if you're provisioning infrastructure, configuring it, and adding application configuration, the pipeline becomes very tightly coupled to the application.

If you begin adding more applications in your organization, your overhead starts to grow quickly. You now need to build and maintain multiple pipelines, each with their own eccentricities. If the platform you build your CI/CD efforts on top of needs to be updated or a new version is released, you may be in the position of rebuilding all your pipelines. This is not an ideal situation to be in, especially if you don't have the staff to handle it.

Bad Actors

Having a single pipeline per application can introduce some bad behavior. Since the pipeline is tied directly to a single codebase, it's not uncommon to receive requests for it to be modified to do nonstandard things. After all, it's a pipeline dedicated to a single application; it must support the needs of the application. If you make a change to it, it only affects this one application. However, these ad hoc changes can quickly put you in a very fragile spot. Take, for instance, the flow as shown in Figure 1-3.

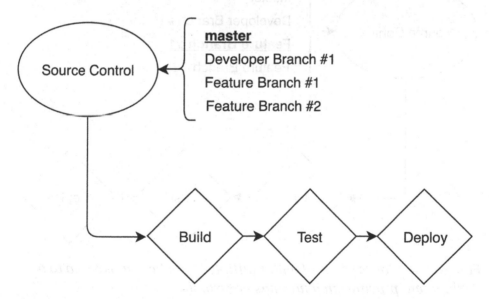

Figure 1-3. *Source control with multiple branches, hooked up to a deployment pipeline*

In this example we have application code stored in source control with multiple branches. The "master" branch is tied to the deployment pipeline. Any commits to "master" will trigger a deployment of the code. Developers can maintain feature or development branches that will eventually get merged into "master." In this scenario "master" is the source of truth, and the only branch that ever gets deployed. This follows proper CI/CD principles and is a very good practice.

As is often the case with larger code bases that have a dedicated pipeline, bad practices begin to emerge. It's not uncommon for a feature branch to become so large that it becomes difficult to easily merge it back into "master." Developers work hard on this branch for an upcoming release, and the clock is ticking. Eventually the request will come down to have the pipeline reconfigured so it points to a feature branch, as shown in Figure 1-4.

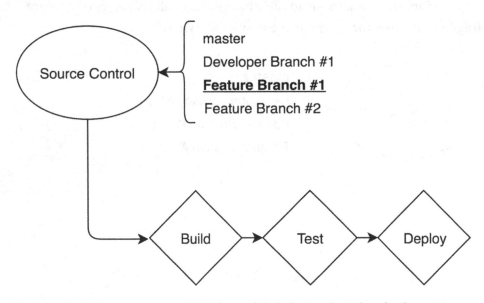

Figure 1-4. *Source control with multiple branches, hooked up to a deployment pipeline on a nonmaster branch*

Now we have our pipeline deploying off a feature branch, which is not good practice. If you have multiple teams working on several features, which branch is now the source of truth? The team is very quickly put into a place where "Feature Branch #1," in this example, is the de facto "master" branch. This very quickly gets out of hand, especially if another team needs to begin working on a new feature at this very moment. They will be forced to create a feature branch off a feature branch!

Another common bad practice is a request to turn off certain stages in the pipeline, as shown in Figure 1-5.

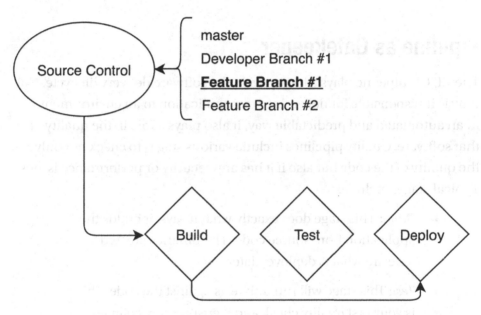

Figure 1-5. *Pipeline that has been configured to bypass unit tests*

Now the pipeline is deploying code that is in a feature branch, and the testing stage has been bypassed. If your pipeline is configured like this, it should raise alarm bells—not for the DevOps team, but for the teams you support. These requests can come over very quickly and are usually the result of tight deadlines, or needing to provide a hotfix for production. Whatever the reason, they introduce risk in the process of delivering quality software. The result most often is that these changes persist past the initial implementation, as technical debt has a way of being created but never resolved.

Info   These examples are from real-world scenarios I've encountered throughout my career. It takes a village to deliver quality software, and the pipeline needs just as much attention at times as your application.

Pipeline as Gatekeeper

The CI/CD pipeline plays a huge role in the software delivery lifecycle. Not only is it responsible for delivering your application to an environment in an automated and predictable way, it also plays a role in the quality of that software. Quality pipelines include various stages to check not only the quality of the code but also if it has any security or performance issues. Typical stages include:

- *Build*: This stage does exactly what it says; it builds the application from source code. The binaries created here are what is deployed later.

- *Test*: This stage will run unit tests against the code. This is your first quality check and it ensures any changes made by the development team did not break expected functionality.

- *Static Code/Security Analysis*: This is a scan of the source files for the application. This scan will look for vulnerabilities, technical debt, and may verify code coverage. This stage could be broken into multiple steps, given your choice of tools to perform the scanning.

- *Storing Artifacts*: A good process takes the binaries created in the Build stage and saves them for later deployments. This ensures that code that was tested and successfully deployed can be promoted later with confidence it passed all your checks.

- *Deployment*: A simple (hopefully) deployment of the binaries to the specified environment, i.e., Dev, QA, Production, etc.

- *End to End/Performance Tests*: Once the code is deployed, you may run automated tests to ensure it performs properly. This can be via a browser or hitting API endpoints. This stage may also be broken up into multiple stages, depending on your needs.

As you can see in this scenario, a CI/CD pipeline can do a lot of work to ensure the code being delivered is a quality product. Bypassing some of these steps is just impossible; you can't deploy if you haven't built the application. However, some could absolutely be skipped, but shouldn't. Teams may find themselves up against tight timelines and realize that their code coverage is beginning to slip. A request may come down to bypass the static code analysis stage. They may import a new code library that has a security vulnerability in it. Rather than address it, another request is received to bypass another stage. Soon you're left with the absolute barebones pipeline.

Note   There is an argument to be made that the CI/CD pipeline is not the place to enforce good behaviors. It's really the responsibility of the development teams to ensure the code is properly tested and secure. However, there is no way to escape the fact that the pipeline is often where these checks are applied.

This behavior is tied directly to the fact that the pipeline serves a single application. The team believes it's in their best interest to ignore some best practices, as they are being pressured to deliver faster. However, if the pipeline is not there as a proper check on what's being deployed, the result could be much worse.

Agile Can't Die; It Was Never Born

CI/CD pipelines are the perfect complement to any team using agile methodologies. In an ideal situation development teams are building features that are committed to source control often. Each commit kicks off a build via the pipeline and your entire test suite is executed. The code is deployed to a lower environment for user acceptance testing, and artifacts are created for later promotion. Once the feature is complete, or maybe the sprint, the new feature is deployed to production and your users are happy.

Even if you're not using agile, these practices still make sense. You want your code built and tested as often as possible. Performing deployments often will also highlight any problems long before you get to push to production. The problem you will most often face is an extremely long lead time to deployment. With a typical monolithic application, the time it takes to deploy from the moment work begins on a new feature can be weeks or months, as shown in Figure 1-6.

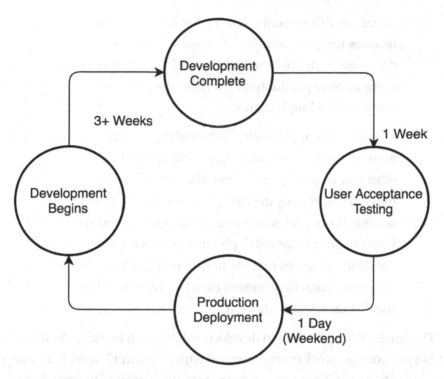

Figure 1-6. *Feature development timeline on a typical monolithic application*

In this example it's over a month from the time development begins on a new feature before it's deployed to production. This cycle time introduces a lot of risk from many different angles:

1. *Developers*: This is one of the main reasons that long-living feature branches exist. Your "master" branch is pristine and you're hesitant to mess with it. However, the long cycle time means your feature branch must also live that long. If multiple features are being developed concurrently, by the time you need to merge back into "master" it becomes a real problem.

2. *Testers*: In this scenario, testers don't see the new features for quite some time. In some cases they don't see compete functionality until the code is ready to go to production. This introduces even more risk if a bug is found.

3. *DevOps*: One of the selling points of pipelines is an automated process that is repeatable; you know what you're getting every time you request a new build. If you're only deploying once a month, that process is not performed enough to become routine. If you're doing manual deployments, this means the subtle nuances that come with that process are forgotten. Each deployment then becomes as if it's the first time you're doing it.

The longer the cycle time to develop and deploy a feature, the more out of sync your feature branch becomes with a "master" branch. In many scenarios changes are being introduced into the "master" branch during this time. UI updates, bug fixes, or other features may get merged. This puts you in a position of merging down from "master" into your feature branch, then merging back up. In either direction you'll most likely encounter conflicts that need to be resolved.

Overview

In this chapter we looked at how a monolithic application with a dedicated pipeline can introduce risk for your deployments. This combination can lead to bad behaviors that often result in cutting corners to meet deadlines. However, it's not all doom and gloom. You can absolutely have a dedicated pipeline that performs all the tasks needed and runs smoothly. This quite often requires strong leaders who are willing to say no to a risky request. The reality is that if the business needs software out the door on a certain date, you do what is required.

In the next chapter we'll look at how microservices can help ease some of these concerns. We'll explore how these services allow you to break away from a dedicated pipeline, into a more standardized approach. You'll begin to see how we can look at the pipeline in more generic ways and get more from your deployments.

CHAPTER 2

Setting the Stage for the Present

When you sat down with this book, you were probably fully caffeinated and ready to dive into learning about the world of generic pipelines. You made it through the introduction and rolled up your sleeves for Chapter 1 when bam, you were served with a healthy dose of "this is how it is." Sorry to rain on your parade, but a lot of companies still work that way. Maybe you are beyond that, on a journey of exploring microservices and how they can improve writing and deploying applications. Alternatively, maybe you work in a shop that is already developing microservices, but struggle with how to manage all the pipelines. It is all very individual, but the good news is we're here to help.

In this chapter we'll begin to explore how you can simplify code deployments using microservices. We'll explore the beginnings of a truly generic pipeline. You'll see how this can improve your agile maturity as well, by lowering risk and delivery time.

Microservices

Microservices represent the true antithesis to monolithic applications. Small and lightweight, these services usually provide specific and very limited functionality. This allows them to focus on singular tasks, which

© Brandon Atkinson, Dallas Edwards 2018
B. Atkinson and D. Edwards, *Generic Pipelines Using Docker*,
https://doi.org/10.1007/978-1-4842-3655-0_2

makes developing them fast, debugging issues easier, and deployments nimbler. A true microservice can be deployed independently of other services and is self-contained. A typical microservice architecture is shown in Figure 2-1.

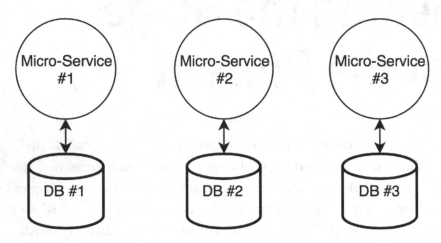

Figure 2-1. *Multiple microservices with dedicated databases*

In this example, each microservice has its own database. This type of architecture allows developers to easily make changes to their services without the need to check with other teams. The service is the source of truth for the data and no other service should manipulate it. If another service needs to get to this data, an API is exposed for that purpose. This way if the developers don't change the API, changes can move forward that don't break other services that consume it. This can also be accomplished with versioned endpoints in the API.

In this architecture, teams can move as fast as they want to and can deploy even faster. Unlike in the monolithic application, which must be deployed as a single unit, microservices can be deployed at different times. This gives teams the flexibility to work on multiple features at the same time, without worrying about stepping on each other's check-ins. Each microservice is in its own repository, so teams are safe to make changes as needed. Adopting microservices is not a magic bullet, however. Teams will need to ensure they use proper API versioning and dependency management.

Note   While microservices can make developers and DevOps lives' easier, they also come with baggage. Usually you end up with a lot of services, since they focus on more singular workloads. This increases your deployments, and the complexity does not necessarily go away. Microservices are not a silver bullet, but they do provide many benefits, which we'll explore in detail.

Developer Best Practices Are Key

One of the tenants of continuous delivery is that teams produce software, or new features, in short cycles. Microservices provide a great way to do this. Since teams can focus solely on their service and adding new features to it, they can move much faster. One of the benefits to this is smaller and quicker check-ins to the "master" branch.

In most cases your deployment pipeline is configured to react to commits to the "master" branch in your source control. A commit will trigger a build, which creates an artifact that can be deployed. Microservices give development teams an opportunity to practice true CI/CD patterns. By this I mean each commit to "master" will trigger a pipeline execution. The pipeline will build, test, and deploy the application each time, all while producing an artifact that can be promoted to Production. Each commit produces a potential production release.

Depending on how mature your organization is, this may seem like madness! Every commit produces a production-ready artifact?! If you're new to microservices, this does sound strange—and even more so if you don't have a sophisticated pipeline. However, consider the following scenario. You are a development team working in agile. You have two-week sprints and plan to produce a feature during each sprint. You have a CI/CD pipeline that performs the following steps:

- Build

- Unit Tests

- Security Scan

- Static Code Analysis

- End to End/Integration Tests

- Artifact Creation

- Deployment

- Performance Tests

In this scenario when your team has finished development and tested locally, they can commit the new feature to the "master" branch in source control. The commit will trigger the pipeline, where a full suite of tests is run to ensure the code is production ready. At the end you have an artifact of the application you can now promote to production. Microservices allow this type of rapid deployment.

While microservices are the gateway to faster release cycles, it takes much more to truly achieve this goal. This architecture gives you isolation from other teams and data stores, which allows for more rapid development. Developers need to ensure their application code is properly unit tested. End to end tests must be written so user acceptance testing can be automated. The same goes for performance tests. Security scans and static code analysis is usually performed by third-party tools, but developers must review the results and potentially update code based on those results.

A great pipeline can get your code deployed in a matter of minutes, fully scanned and tested. However, it's a team effort to build production-ready code. Simply developing the application is no longer enough. Proper testing and scanning must be in place to ensure the application being deployed works and is safe for your business.

Note   There is debate about how small or large a microservice should be. Should it cover all the possible needs of a certain business process, for instance "Billing"? Or, should it be much more granular, for instance one for "Send Bill" and another for "Process Payment". At the end of the day, this is a business decision. However, a good rule of thumb is if you can't re-build it in a sprint (roughly 2-3 weeks), then it's too big.

Dedicated Pipeline per Language

Microservices give us a better way of delivering application code. In the previous chapter we looked at how a monolithic application has a dedicated pipeline for the application itself. Let's review what the application looked like, as shown in Figure 2-2.

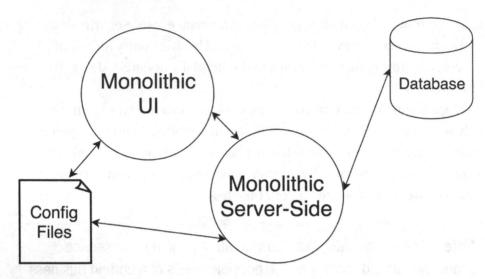

Figure 2-2. *Monolith application*

While this application is a monolith, it would most likely have three
pipelines to deploy it: one for the server-side application, one for the UI,
and one for the database. Even though you have split the deployment
into three components, they are all still tied to a single application. There
is little to no reuse of code in those pipelines. Microservices provide
an opportunity to improve this. Most business applications will have
some sort of UI. Let's look at an example business application that uses
microservices, as shown in Figure 2-3.

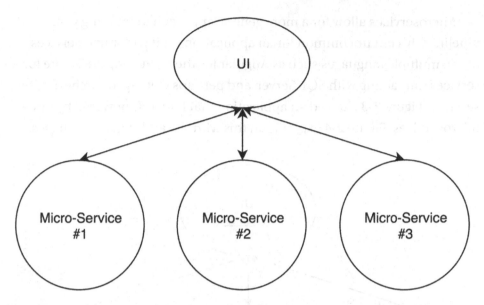

Figure 2-3. *Application that uses microservices with a UI*

In this scenario we still have a UI that users interact with, but now the business logic is separated out into multiple microservices. As more functionality is added, more microservices are added as well. Following the monolithic approach, we'd build a pipeline per UI and/or microservice. This may be OK if you only plan on having a few services, but what happens if your application and business take off and you end up with a dozen microservices. What about 20, 50, or 100? You may think those numbers are high, but you'll be surprised at how fast adoption grows once you start down the microservices path.

Caution   Don't take for granted how fast microservice adoption can take place or how many services you may end up with. Netflix runs hundreds of microservices to power its operation, reportedly over 500. You can be assured they do not have dedicated pipelines for each service.

Microservices allow for a more generic approach to building your pipelines. It's not uncommon for an application built with microservices to use multiple languages such as Angular for the front end, .NET Core for services interacting with SQL Server, and perhaps Golang for orchestration services. Figure 2-3 showed an application that had a UI powered by three microservices. Figure 2-4 expands on this with the addition of languages.

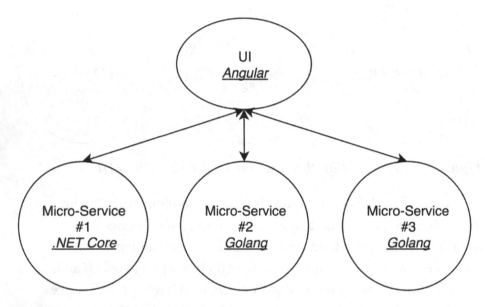

Figure 2-4. *Application that uses microservices with a UI, with languages added for reference*

In this example our UI is Angular, but it could be React or something similar. We have a .NET Core service and two Golang services. The languages here are not important at all. You can easily substitute Java for .NET, or Python for Golang. Whatever language is prominent in your organization, you can count on microservices written in it, plus at least one more. One of the benefits microservices provide is the ability to choose the language that is right for the job. As mentioned, you may want to use .NET to interact with SQL Server due to its frameworks custom built for that purpose. You may choose Golang as an orchestration service due to its speed and small footprint. You may choose an entirely different language simply because you have a shop full of developers who already know it. The list goes on and on. However, as you build your pipelines you must be prepared for a new language popping up at any time.

Now that we are looking at applications built with one or more languages, we can start to look at the pipeline as being language specific rather than application specific. This is beneficial for a variety of reasons, including:

- *Faster on-boarding*: If your pipeline is built for a language rather than a specific application, others can use it if they write their applications in the same language. Teams can on-board to the pipeline faster and begin providing business value much sooner.

- *Reuse of code*: You're not spending your time writing custom code for each application. Your pipeline code is reused across multiple applications.

- *Ease of maintenance*: If a new feature is required of the pipeline or you need to perform a bug fix, everyone gets those changes. Imagine you have an Angular 4 pipeline and Angular 5 is released. Simply update your Angular pipeline, and all UIs benefit at the same time.

Language-specific pipelines provide a lot of code reuse, which will make your life easier. This becomes very apparent once you build out a language-specific pipeline and teams begin to on-board. In the monolith world, a team would build an application and put in a request for a new pipeline. With language-specific pipelines built for microservices, you can build it once, then simply have teams utilize it. Figure 2-5 illustrates this concept.

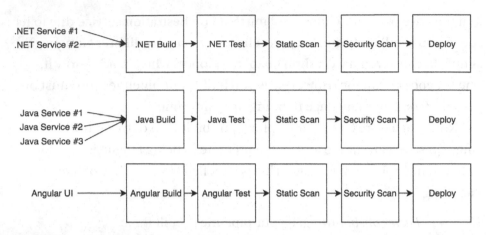

Figure 2-5. *Multiple services and UIs utilizing language-specific pipelines*

Now you're no longer writing and rewriting code for your pipelines. Teams using the same language will also use the same pipeline. However, this can only be achieved with proper standards in place. Everyone must agree on a certain baseline set of rules and patterns that the pipeline will follow. You can't have shared pipelines if everyone wants to do something different.

Note   Examples that show .NET or .NET Core are referencing .NET Core running on Linux. One of the benefits of shared pipelines is they all run in Linux environments, and usually the same environment. Not jumping between Windows and Linux is a true benefit here, and you should take advantage of it.

Standards Are Key

We'll be exploring standards much more in depth later in the book as we begin to take shared pipelines even further. However, it's an important area that we'll look at now because it's crucial to making these pipelines work. We'll scratch the surface now, and in future chapters we'll really dig in.

In the previous section we talked about the need for consensus on how things work in the pipeline. For a shared pipeline to function correctly for all, a few key standards must be defined:

- How you build

- How you test

- How you deploy

Some of these may seem trivial, but once you begin working with multiple teams you'll find folks have their own ways of doing things. It's important that the pipeline performs the exact same commands for all applications for a specific language. Take .NET Core as an example: you may settle on the build command shown in Listing 2-1.

Listing 2-1. .NET Core Build Command

```
dotnet build -c Release -o /build-output
```

This command will build the application in the current directory in Release (Production) mode and store the binaries in an output folder called "build-output." Listing 2-2 shows an example test command.

Listing 2-2. .Net Core Test Command

```
dotnet test -c Release -o /build-output
```

This command will unit test the application in the current directory in Release (Production) mode and look for binaries in the folder named "build-output." Both commands are perfectly fine and would run without any issues. However, what if you have a development team that wants to run a dotnet build command, but with different arguments? Or you have a request not to build in "Release" mode, but rather in "Debug" mode? If you accommodate each team's request, your pipeline will need to react differently based on the code it is building and testing. If you're dealing with dozens of services, this would not be sustainable.

The goal of a shared pipeline is to greatly decrease cycle time and release code faster. To do this the pipeline must be opinionated, in that it runs certain commands and only those commands. If a team wishes to deploy their application with your pipeline, they must play by the rules. At first glance this does not seem like a huge ask of your development teams. However, you may find that opinions differ on the best way to build and test applications. People may have certain tools or patterns they prefer over others. The key is getting a standard in place and sticking to it.

The best way to accomplish this is to interview your developers. Find out exactly which commands they run locally to build and test. In most cases you'll find the commands are the same or differ only slightly. Once you have this information, you can work with the teams to settle on the standard commands the pipeline will run. After that, all teams must agree to use these commands going forward. This is the easy part, as you enforce those via the pipeline. If the application cannot be built and tested using the standard commands, it won't be deployed.

Taking Code Reuse a Step Further

Once you have a language-specific pipeline in place, you may notice that some of your steps are identical. These tend to be tasks dedicated to various things like security scans or static code analysis. Submitting code for scans usually involves zipping up the source code or binaries, and uploading them to a service that performs the scan. There are many commercial platforms and software packages that perform static code and security analysis. They usually work with a long list of languages. What this means for your pipeline is a generic step that any language can use. Figure 2-6 illustrates a shared step across all your pipelines.

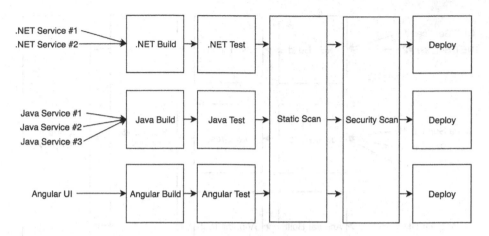

Figure 2-6. *Code reuse across common areas*

As you can see, not only are we pushing more applications through fewer pipelines, now we're beginning to reuse code across pipelines as well. This illustration should begin to solidify how shared pipelines can reduce your workload. This also illustrates how generic steps can be utilized anywhere you need them.

Now, let's assume that your pipeline is using static code analysis for code quality. Let's also assume the business has decided to utilize containers and the cloud for deployments. Your pipeline can be further simplified, as shown in Figure 2-7. With these changes you can share even more code across multiple pipelines. Uploading code for a static code analysis and deploying to the cloud are not trivial matters. However, the underlying mechanics don't change very much between applications. Some simple configuration data is all that is needed for each of these steps to operate properly.

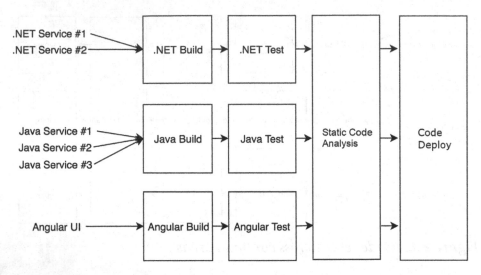

Figure 2-7. *Pipeline utilizing shared steps for static code analysis and cloud deploy*

In this example half of the pipeline is now shared code. The only steps that are not generic are the ones tied directly to a language like build and unit test. As your development practices begin to mature, you'll find additional steps that can be shared, like performance testing, artifact storage, logging, etc. The idea with this pattern is to make steps as generic as possible.

Most CI/CD platforms allow for code reuse either directly or indirectly. Jenkins, for instance, allows you to pull in code from various repositories. Circle CI and Drone CI allow you to configure scripts to run for each step, which can easily be reused. This code reuse provides so many benefits as your microservices begin to grow. The more code you can reuse the better off you'll be.

Microservices and Shared Pipelines are More Agile

Whether you like agile practices or hate them, they provide a process to release code much faster. Microservices and shared pipelines can greatly facilitate this process. With microservices you can begin to focus on smaller releases, generally tied around a new feature. Figure 2-8 illustrates a release cycle of two weeks, which could match up to the development team's sprint.

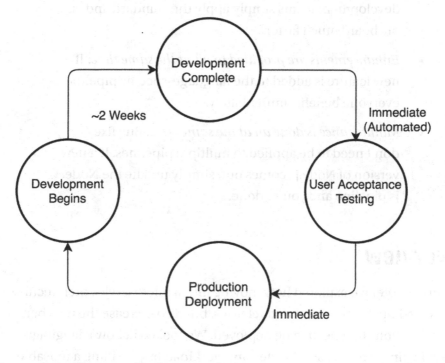

Figure 2-8. *Two-week release cycle*

As the example demonstrates, development takes approximately two weeks, at which point the feature code is committed to the "master" branch. The pipeline is executed based on the commit and a full suite of tests are kicked off. A release candidate artifact is created and can be promoted to Production at any time. This image looks drastically different than the one shown in the previous chapter. Microservices give you the opportunity for rapid development, testing, and deployments.

A shared pipeline by itself does not necessarily contribute to rapid deployments. It's the benefits of this pattern where you see the speed:

- *Teams can on-board faster*: Gone are the days of requesting a custom pipeline, meeting to discuss needs, and waiting for it to be built and tested. Now development teams simply apply the standard and can on-board much faster.

- *Enhancements are provided to all at the same time*: If a new feature is added to the language-specific pipeline, everyone benefits immediately.

- *Maintenance is done all at the same time*: Bug fixes don't need to be applied to multiple pipelines. If a new version of Node.js comes out, simply update the Node. js pipeline and you're done.

Overview

In this chapter we explored how moving into a microservice architecture can speed up development and releases, but also increase the number of applications that need to be deployed. We looked at how a language-specific pipeline can ease the DevOps workload by providing a reusable shared pipeline that all teams can use. We also reviewed how code reuse is possible in this pattern, further lightening the load and increasing output.

In the next chapter we'll go one step further, and begin exploring the truly generic pipeline. Not only generic from the application's point of view but also from the underlying platform perspective. We'll see how Docker can help us take our pipelines anywhere and how scripts take code reuse to the next level.

CHAPTER 3

Getting it Right with Docker and Scripts

Up until now we've looked at pipelines that work with monoliths and microservices. We've explored the challenges that come with both, but have seen how microservices can ease your pipeline workload. In the previous chapter we saw how you can build language-specific pipelines. These implementations allow for multiple teams to take advantage of a single pipeline. It also makes you begin to set and enforce development standards, which allows for code reuse across your pipelines. We'll explore this concept much deeper in later chapters with code examples.

Language specific pipelines are great; they allow the DevOps team to focus on fewer pipelines by giving feature teams a shared implementation. It lowers maintenance efforts, allows for all teams to share in upgrades and improvements, and sets standards for how applications are deployed. While all this is great, we can do better. Imagine if you could build a single pipeline that could deploy any application regardless of the language it was written in. How much time could your DevOps team get back if they only had to support one implementation?

In this chapter we'll begin laying the foundations of the generic pipeline using Docker. You'll learn the pattern and process that allows a truly generic pipeline to work. We'll explore how this pattern is driven by Docker and frees you from the underlying platform the pipeline runs on. At the end of this chapter you'll be ready to start coding an implementation.

© Brandon Atkinson, Dallas Edwards 2018
B. Atkinson and D. Edwards, *Generic Pipelines Using Docker*,
https://doi.org/10.1007/978-1-4842-3655-0_3

One Pipeline to Rule Them All

Language-specific pipelines are a great first start. They allow you to break free of application-specific implementations and begin to serve a larger base of teams simultaneously. However, as your feature teams begin to fully embrace microservices, it stands to reason they will begin to embrace other languages as well. You may start off as a 100% .NET or Java shop, and slowly turn into a true polyglot shop. This may not be a huge concern if you're supporting a few languages, but what about five, six, or seven languages? This may seem like a lot, but it's not. I have worked at organizations that had the following languages to support:

- *User Interface*: Angular and React

- *Server Side*: .NET Core, Java, Node.js, Python, Golang

Microservices give feature teams the flexibility to try out new languages and patterns. They allow for choosing the right language for the job as well. Take .NET and SQL Server for instance. Let's imagine you've been writing back-end services in Node.js and now must write a new API that connects to SQL Server. You could use Node.js for this task; however, .NET has built-in functionality to do just that. You can very quickly spin up a .NET Core microservice that handles CRUD operations against your SQL Server. It would be faster to write and less error prone, since it's inside the .NET ecosystem.

Another scenario involves hiring of new talent. Suppose you hire an amazing developer. When they join, they talk about writing their microservices in Golang, since it's easy to write, easy to learn, and compiles and deploys very fast. You try it out and like it. Suddenly Golang services are springing up all over the place. The moral of the story is with microservices developers, feel free to try out new languages or stray from the standard if another language provides benefits.

As more and more languages come on the scene, you'll find yourself writing more and more pipeline implementations. If you're in an organization that supports seven languages, that would be seven pipelines.

Even in a simple scenario, you'd have two languages to support, one for the UI and one for the server side. That's one too many! A better solution is a single pipeline that is built to handle any language that your teams work with.

In the previous chapter we looked at shared steps of a pipeline, as shown in Figure 3-1.

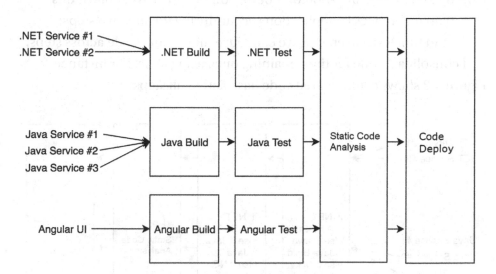

Figure 3-1. *Shared steps of a CI/CD pipeline*

A typical pipeline may consist of the following steps:

- Build

- Unit Test

- Static Code Scan/Security Scan

- Packaging/Publishing of Artifacts

- Deploying

- End to End Tests

- Performance Tests

How mature your organization and CI/CD efforts will determine how many steps you have, but these are a good target. Upon close examination, most of these steps are not specific to a language. For instance, if you're using commercial software for static code analysis it will usually work with a wide variety of languages. Packaging of artifacts usually involves zipping up binaries and shouldn't be any different across applications. The main differences in applications occur during the first two steps: build and unit test. Given this, we can reuse most of our code across steps, and consolidate code for the remaining ones using logic. For instance, Figure 3-2 shows a fully shared code base across all steps.

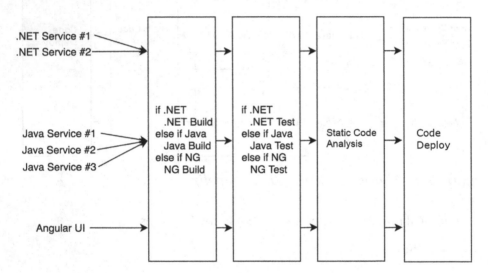

Figure 3-2. *Pipeline stages using shared code*

In this scenario, the entire pipeline is now shared across all languages. Logic is included in the language-specific steps to perform the appropriate commands. This can be accomplished via if/else blocks, switch/case statements, etc. At first glance this may seem like a lot of logic code, especially if you're dealing with a lot of languages. However, earlier in the book we discussed implementing development standards in your shared pipeline. In this scenario you'd have set common build commands to run for each language. For instance, in .NET you'd use the standard "dotnet build" command. These commands generally will be the built-in, out of the box commands for each language. The goal is to set a standard that all teams can follow without being overly complicated. Listing 3-1 shows an example build step.

Listing 3-1. Sample Build Step in a Generic Pipeline

```
if [ $language = "dotnetcore" ]
then
    dotnet build -c Release -o /output
elif [ $language = "java" ]
then
    mvn package -s settings.xml -f /
elif [ $language = "angular" ]
then
    npm run build
else
    echo "Error: No valid language provided."
fi
```

This example shows how you can pass in a simple variable, "language" in this case, to inform the step which language it is working with. An if/else statement then allows you to perform the build command for that language. Listing 3-2 shows the same example using a switch/case statement.

Listing 3-2. Sample Build Step Using a Switch/Case Statement

```
case $language in
"dotnetcore")
      dotnet build -c Release -o /output
      ;;
"java")
      mvn package -s settings.xml -f /
      ;;
"angular")
      npm run build
      ;;
*)
      echo "Error: No valid language provided."
      ;;
esac
```

In this example we're covering three languages in the "build" step: Angular, .NET Core, and Java. The commands in each section are admittedly short and probably not a full set of the commands you may run. For instance, a proper Angular build section may look more like Listing 3-3.

Listing 3-3. A More Complete Angular Build Step

```
"angular")
      npm set progress=false
      npm install --registry https://registry.npmjs.org/
      npm run build
      ;;
```

This case statement has three times the amount of code in it, but it's still small for all intents and purposes. Even if you need to do more complex things for a specific language, you will most likely not end up with so many lines that it's unmanageable. This is where setting standards for languages becomes important. To build a truly language-agnostic pipeline that all teams can use, you need high-quality standards. We'll continue to explore this throughout the book; however, in this case your Angular build standard would be:

- Run "npm set progress=false" to turn off progress bars.

- Run "npm install" to restore packages.

- Run "npm build" to build the project.

- No other commands will be run.

With this build standard in place, all teams would need to conform to it or in order to use your pipeline. This may seem harsh, but there are a lot of benefits to it. Teams that share common standards on how they build and test can more rapidly debug issues and assist other teams with issues, and it simplifies your work in the pipeline. Now of course, there will always be outliers who need to do things their own way. In those cases it's important not to deviate from the standard. You could explore things like a custom pipeline for that application, or provide hooks into the pipeline to allow teams to override your steps. In most cases you will need to hold strong on the standards and say no to a lot of requests.

Shell Scripts

For your pipeline to be truly generic and run anywhere, it needs to be written in a way that is portable. So far we've explored writing shared steps. In the previous section we saw how to combine commands from different languages into a single step. In case you haven't noticed, those commands were all written in Shell. For this book we've chosen Shell scripts to execute all our commands.

Shell scripts were an easy choice to make for a variety of reasons. All our examples are written in languages that run in a Linux environment. This includes .NET Core, Angular, and Java. This was also an easy choice, since this book is about writing pipelines with Docker. While Docker can run on Windows, I would argue most organizations don't utilize this option—especially those running on Amazon Web Services using Elastic Container Service (ECS) or Google Cloud Platform Kubernetes Engine. A Shell environment will be present in all our containers without any additional installations, which is nice!

No matter the container we're working in, we're confident a Shell environment is available. However, this is not the case with all Shell languages. Bash, for instance, is a very popular Shell language, but if you're new to Docker you'll quickly find out that it's not always available. For instance, Alpine containers, which are lightweight Linux distribution based on "musl libc" and "busybox", have a Shell environment but do not come with Bash installed.

While we have chosen Shell scripts for this book, there is no reason you cannot deviate from this and use another scripting language. For instance, you can use Bash or Python just as easily. The only caveat is you will need to ensure those runtimes are installed in your Docker image. In fact, if you happen to be using Windows containers, there is no reason you can't follow along with us. You'll just be using PowerShell in your containers, most likely.

Let's take the example from the previous section and reimagine it as a Shell script for the build step. Listing 3-4 shows what this might look like.

Listing 3-4. Build Step as a Shell Script

```
#!/usr/bin/env sh

case $1 in
"dotnetcore")
        dotnet build -c Release -o /output
        ;;
"java")
        mvn package -s settings.xml -f /
        ;;
"angular")
        npm run build
        ;;
*)
        echo "Error: No valid language provided."
        ;;
esac
```

This example looks almost identical to Listing 3-2, with a couple of small but important changes. First, we've include a shebang as the first line in the file to indicate this is a Shell script. This would change based on the language you're using. For instance, if you wanted to use Python 3 your shebang would be #!/usr/bin/python3. Next, we've replaced the "$language" variable with a "$1" indicating we're passing it in as an argument. While this is still a very simple implementation of a build step, these two changes make it a fully functional step. Just save it as "build.sh" and you're ready to use it in your pipeline.

This also opens the door for making your pipeline logic much more modular. Take Listing 3-3 as an example. This was a much more detailed build command for Angular. Granted it is all of three lines, but imagine you have a language that requires 30 lines or more. This is probably more code than you care to have in a switch/case statement. Now that we're using Shell scripts, we can reimagine that code as a separate script as shown in Listing 3-5.

Listing 3-5. Angular Build Commands in Their Own Shell Script

```sh
#!/usr/bin/env sh

npm set progress=false
npm install --registry https://registry.npmjs.org/
npm run build
```

Now, this script can be saved as "angular_build.sh". All your build logic is now consolidated into a separate script. If you needed to go crazy and have dozens of lines of code, it's isolated here. This makes writing, maintenance, and debugging much easier. It also begins to open the door for sharing code across multiple pipelines. If we take all our build commands and put them into separate Shell scripts, our build step could be simplified as shown in Listing 3-6.

Listing 3-6. Simplified Build Step Shell Script

```sh
#!/usr/bin/env sh

case $1 in
"dotnetcore")
      dotnet_build.sh
      ;;
"java")
      maven_build.sh
      ;;
"angular")
      angular_build.sh
      ;;
*)
```

```
    echo "Error: No valid language provided."
    ;;
esac
```

While we haven't reduced the line count of the code in the file, we've greatly simplified it, making it easier to read and follow. The script is no longer cluttered with code from the various languages. If we need to add another language, simply write the appropriate build script and then add another case statement to the build step script.

This method introduces shared scripts that can be executed from a step on your CI/CD platform. For instance, let's imagine that you have multiple lines of business in your organization, each with their own DevOps team. Each LOB has development teams building microservices, and each runs their own CI/CD platform. We'll also say that all those teams are writing microservices in Node.js. It's not hard to imagine that each DevOps group has its own pipeline that can build, test, and deploy Node.js services. Each pipeline is essentially doing the same thing, and most likely using almost identical code to do it!

If both teams adopted using Shell scripts to build their Node.js services, then they could then easily share code. In fact, the code in Listing 3-5 could simply be renamed "npm_build.sh" and used for all Node.js applications! Even if each team was using different platforms for their pipelines, running Shell scripts is supported in every major platform.

Configuration Files

For Shell scripts to properly handle multiple languages, you must have some way to inform your pipeline about the application you want to build. You want to be explicit about what you are doing. A configuration file can solve this issue for you. Development teams can place this file in their repo and it would be cloned along with the application when the pipeline executes. It would contain all the information the pipeline would need to execute. Listing 3-7 shows what a simple configuration file may look like.

> **Note**   This book focuses on building applications that are deployed
> via Docker containers to an orchestration service like Amazon ECS
> or Kubernetes. As such, the configuration file shown in this chapter
> is specific to that. A configuration file for your applications may look
> drastically different.

Listing 3-7. A Sample Configuration File

```
{
  "application": {
    "name": "Hello App",
    "language": "dotnetcore"
  },
  "build": {
    "path": "",
    "outputPath": "HelloApp/bin/Release/netcoreapp2.0"
  },
  "test": {
    "enabled": true,
    "path": "HelloTests/"
  },
  "archive": {
    "registry": "docker.io",
    "namespace": "YOUR-NAMESPACE",
    "repository": "YOUR-REPO"
  },
  "deploy": {
    "containerPort": 5000
  }
}
```

Let's break this down by each section to better understand its makeup:

- *Application*: Contains basic information about the application

  - *Name*: This is a friendly name for the application. This may be its identifier in the UI of the platform or used for reporting.

  - *Language*: This is the language the application is written in. This is the most important, if not only, variable the pipeline may care about.

- *Build*: Contains information about how to build the application

  - *Path*: This would be the directory path in the cloned repo, in case your application is located somewhere other than root.

  - *OutputPath*: This tells the pipeline where the built binaries should be placed. It is useful if other stages require the binaries to be placed in specific locations.

- *Tests*: Contains information about how to execute unit tests

  - *Enabled*: Would allow the application to bypass a stage

  - *Path*: Used if the unit tests are not located in the same directory as the application

- *Archive*: Contains information about how to archive the built application

  - *Registry*: The URL to the Docker registry where the application will be pushed

  - *Namespace*: The namespace in the registry

  - *Repository*: The repository name under the namespace

- *Deploy*: Contains information pertaining to the deployment

  - *ContainerPort*: The container port number

As you can see, even a simple configuration file can get complex very fast. However, this file contains just enough information that our pipeline can execute its stages and deploy our application. A lot of thought needs to go into these files to make them flexible for future changes. Additional sections may include things like:

- Security Scans

- Static Code Analysis

- Performance Tests

- ATDD Tests

This could go on and on. The main takeaway here is that for a generic pipeline that uses shared code to function properly, you need a way to instruct it on which paths to take while executing. We will explore configuration files in more detail, as well as use them in later chapters.

Docker at the Core

At the core of the generic pipeline is Docker. It is the glue that holds everything together, as well as the magic that makes it all possible. Docker provides a mechanism where we can isolate our pipeline from the underlying platform. It also allows us to create an environment that is specific to the needs of the application being deployed. For instance, if we're building a .NET Core application, we don't need to worry about having the Java runtime installed. It also allows for us to easily target specific runtime.

If you're in a larger organization, it's not uncommon to have an enterprise CI/CD platform that you must use. In these scenarios you are often forced to use the runtimes that are installed on the platform, or face long lead times to get new ones installed. Continuing with our .NET Core example, imagine we have an enterprise platform with various runtimes installed:

- Java Runtime Environment 8

- .NET Core 1.0

- Python 2.6

- .NET Standard 4.5

- Sonar Scanner 2.0

If we're using .NET Core 1.0 we're in good shape. It's installed on the platform, and we can build and deploy to our heart's content. Figure 3-3 shows what this platform may look like.

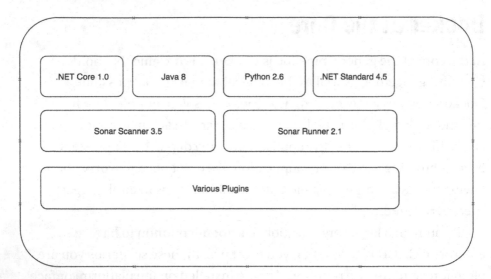

Figure 3-3. *Enterprise CI/CD platform*

Things are humming along just fine; however, our development
team has begun working on a new version of their application and they
are using .NET Core 2.0. Well that's not going to work; we need to get
.NET Core upgraded on the platform. In most cases this is not a quick
process. For an enterprise to run a tight ship, they need to vet installations
in lower environments first. Only after proper testing has taken place
can the upgraded version of the runtime be scheduled for a Production
deployment. That also takes time, as you need to secure a change order
and downtime window. Figure 3-4 shows the updated platform after the
installation.

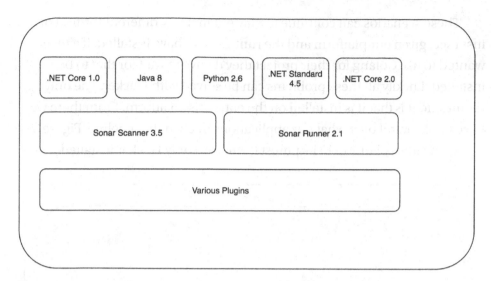

Figure 3-4. *Enterprise CI/CD platform with new runtimes installed*

If your team happens to be agile, they are most likely putting you on their impediment list! At this point the enterprise platform has become a bottleneck slowing down the development teams. In a worst-case scenario, you're stifling progress and innovation because teams cannot move as fast as they need to. Imagine that an early access release of .NET Core comes out and a team would like to use it for their application. This would be even more of a challenge given it's not a release candidate!

In addition to the slowdowns that this can present, there are also a ton of runtimes installed that most developers don't need. To put it another way, the Java developers don't need .NET Core and vice versa. Now most of the time this is not a problem, as multiple runtimes can be installed side by side without issue. But larger platforms, like Jenkins, also come with a lot of plugins that sometimes don't play nice with each other. As the platform's popularity grows inside the organization, more and more requests for plugins flow in. At some point there may be a conflict between plugins, and someone will have to lose out on functionality they were counting on.

These scenarios can continue to play out in many different forms. For instance, given our platform and the runtimes we have installed, if a team wanted to use Golang for their project they'd have to wait for that to be installed. Luckily all these problems can be solved with Docker. The only requirement is that it is installed on the enterprise platform. From there we have total control over what our applications need in the pipeline. Figure 3-5 shows the ideal platform in its purest form, with only Docker installed.

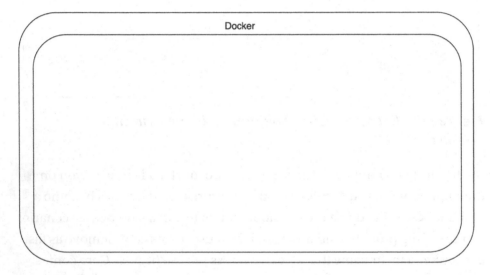

Figure 3-5. *Enterprise CI/CD platform with only Docker installed*

Now at this point you may be thinking to yourself, "this is insane." Why would I have an entire platform and only put Docker on it. Well, you're still going to have a lot of other things installed/configured for your enterprise. However, you can begin to break free of installing individual runtimes and tooling to support all the applications your platform supports. Docker allows for teams to control their environments and only install things specific to their applications.

In the previous figures we had a platform with many runtimes installed to support many different development teams. Let's see what that looks like with Docker in the mix. Figure 3-6 shows the platform once we begin to utilize Docker.

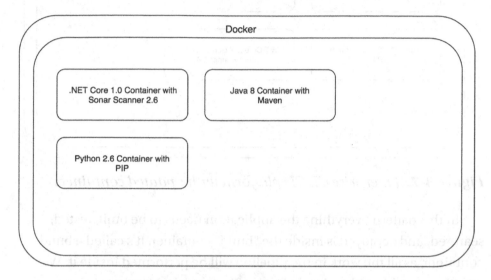

Figure 3-6. *Enterprise CI/CD platform utilizing Docker during builds*

In this scenario, each application is built, tested, and deployed inside a container that is isolated from other containers. The container is responsible for what components and runtimes are installed, thus relieving the platform team of being responsible for installing and maintaining multiple runtimes on the platform. With this approach, the previous scenario of a team switching to a new runtime version becomes trivial. In fact, a team wanting to be bleeding edge and use an Early Access release is not a concern for the enterprise platform team anymore. Figure 3-7 shows an updated .NET Core 2.0 container and an Early Access .NET Core container being utilized.

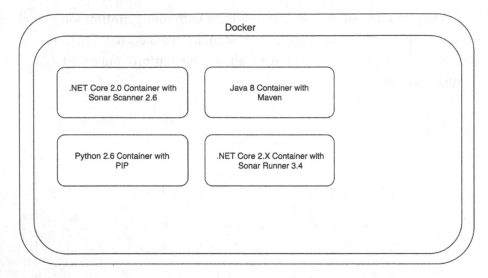

Figure 3-7. *Enterprise CI/CD platform with updated containers*

In this pattern everything the application needs to be built, tested, scanned, and deployed is inside the "build" container. It's called a build container, as all the work in the pipeline will be performed inside it. We can illustrate this with a simple Dockerfile example. Listing 3-8 shows a sample Dockerfile for a .NET Core 1.0 application.

Listing 3-8. Sample Dockerfile for a .NET Core 1.0 Build Container

```
FROM microsoft/1.0-runtime:latest
RUN apt-get update && apt-get install -y \
        unzip
RUN wget http://repo1.maven.org/.../sonar-runner-dist-2.4.zip && \
        unzip sonar-runner-dist-2.4.zip -d /opt
ENV PATH $PATH:/opt/sonar-runner-dist-2.4/bin
```

In this example our build container is based on a .NET Core base image. We update "apt-get" and install "unzip". After that we download Sonar Runner, unzip it, and update the "PATH" so we can easily run it.

At this point we have a build container that can build, test, and scan .NET Core 1.0 applications. Now if the development team decides they want to move to .NET Core 2.0 (why wouldn't they) we simply create another build container using the Dockerfile shown in Listing 3-9.

Listing 3-9. Sample Dockerfile for a .NET Core 2.0 Build Container

```
FROM microsoft/aspnetcore-build:2.0
RUN apt-get update && apt-get install -y \
        unzip
RUN wget http://repo1.maven.org/.../sonar-runner-dist-2.4.zip && \
        unzip sonar-runner-dist-2.4.zip -d /opt
ENV PATH $PATH:/opt/sonar-runner-dist-2.4/bin
```

As you can see, the only thing that changed was the base image of the Dockerfile. In this scenario we now have two build containers, all from changing a single line of code. Contrast that with what it would take to install a new runtime in the platform, fully test it in lower environments, and then promote it to Production. With Docker, we can simply make a change to a Dockerfile and test it. If it works, great! If not, you've literally wasted about ten minutes of work.

Earlier in the chapter we saw an example architecture where the pipeline was made up of shared components. Figure 3-8 shows us this concept again.

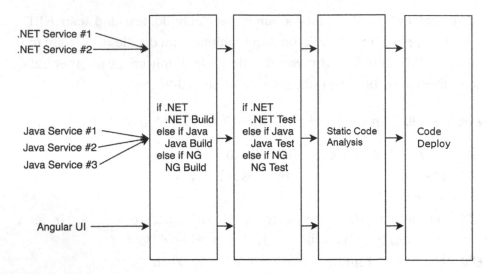

Figure 3-8. *Pipeline stages using shared code*

In this scenario we used Shell scripts to encapsulate shared commands, which can be used across all of the application deployments. Now, we can envision this taking place inside Docker containers, as shown in Figure 3-9.

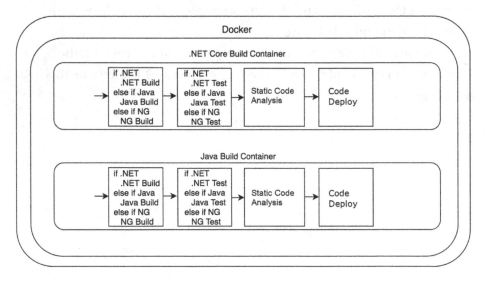

Figure 3-9. *Pipeline stages using shared code inside build containers*

Now we have common shared pipeline code loaded into build containers that are isolated from each other. The same code is copied into each container, but changes to a container no longer have any side effects on the others. This is drastically different than if the CI/CD platform is responsible for all the runtimes and plugins. As illustrated earlier, a team can quickly and safely jump to a new version of a runtime without fear of affecting other teams on the previous runtime. Loading the shared shell scripts is extremely easy. All we need to do is add a COPY command to our build container Dockerfile, as shown in Listing 3-10.

Listing 3-10. Adding Shell Scripts to Our Build Container

```
FROM microsoft/aspnetcore-build:2.0
COPY stages stages
RUN apt-get update && apt-get install -y \
        unzip
RUN wget http://repo1.maven.org/.../sonar-runner-dist-2.4.zip && \
        unzip sonar-runner-dist-2.4.zip -d /opt
ENV PATH $PATH:/opt/sonar-runner-dist-2.4/bin
```

In this example we assume there is a directory called "stages" that holds all the Shell scripts for our pipeline. By copying the scripts into each build container, we have further isolated changes they may impact other teams. A change to a script will only be reflected once the build container is rebuilt. This is certainly not the only way to get your shell scripts into your build container. You could copy them in as part of an application clone, or if using a language like Python you could include them as modules and perform a PIP installation. The main takeaway is that the scripts are part of the build container and isolated from other code.

Platform Agnostic

Running a CI/CD pipeline inside a Docker container provides you with so many benefits. We've already seen how it can provide your development teams isolation from other runtimes, and give them total flexibility on what is installed in the container. Combine this with scripts loaded into the container to execute your pipeline code, and now you're decoupled from the underlying platform. This is a very big deal.

Many enterprise grade CI/CD platforms already allow you to share code across pipelines; this is not a new concept. However, in most cases the mechanisms in place to do so are clunky and not ideal. Take for instance Jenkins, which is a very large player in this space. Jenkins allows you to configure libraries that contain shared code for use in your pipeline. These can be configured at the local (folder) level or globally. Figure 3-10 shows a sample configuration.

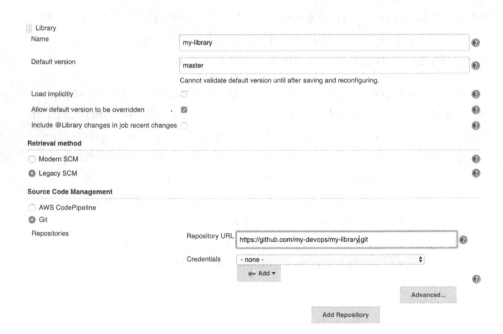

Figure 3-10. *Folder level configuration of a shared library*

In this scenario, we have a GitHub repo called "my-library" with some shared code in it. We reference this library in our Jenkinsfile for the pipeline to load it. Jenkins has a very specific directory structure to allow these files to be shared. The "my-library" repo would be structured like Listing 3-11.

Listing 3-11. Directory Structure of a Shared Library

```
(root - "my-library")
+- vars
|    +- foo.groovy
|    +- bar.groovy
|    +- baz.groovy
```

There may be many more files in this directory but there must be a folder named "vars," which only contains Groovy files. While this is a fine method for sharing code across pipelines, it leaves a lot to be desired. This pattern also makes roper unit testing of the code more difficult, albeit still possible. It also locks us into using Groovy for our shared code, or at least using it as an entry point and then calling something else under the covers.

By using more generic scripts like Shell, we can already begin to break free of the platform even without Docker in the equation. If you're on Windows you can use PowerShell, or even now you can consider Bash, which would not only decouple you from the platform but also the operating system. Putting Docker into the mix gives you the same capability; the only requirement now is that Docker be installed. You could also explore a language like Python, which pretty much runs anywhere.

If we were to move all the code in "my-library" into Shell scripts, our Jenkins configuration would be much simpler. In fact, all the steps from earlier would be gone. We'd have a Docker container loaded with our scripts, which we would simply run on Jenkins. Listing 3-12 shows a sample Docker image run in Jenkins. This example is in Groovy, and the Jenkins platform has the Docker plugin installed.

Listing 3-12. Running a Docker cContainer in Jenkins

```
docker.withRegistry('YOUR-DOCKER-REGISTRY') {
      docker.image('YOUR-CUSTOM-IMAGE').inside('ARGS') {
            stage('Clone') {
                  sh("/stages/01_clone.sh")
            }
            stage('Build') {
                  sh("/stages/02_build.sh")
            }
            stage("Test") {
                  sh("/stages/03_test.sh")
            }
            stage("Archive") {
                  sh("/stages/04_archive.sh")
            }
      }
}
```

Note   The preceding stages are the actual stages we'll be building in upcoming chapters. This example would assume that you have cloned or copied your scripts into the root of the container that is mapped to the Jenkins workspace.

Now that we have all our shared code in scripts in a GitHub repo, we can copy that in via our Dockerfile and use the preceding command to execute the container. You have the option to either "bake" your scripts into the container when it's built, or you could even do a git clone command to bring the scripts down when the container runs. The point here is you have some options.

Now let's consider that you have your pipeline built in a Docker container using Shell scripts, and you're up and running on Jenkins. Everything is going great, and then your boss comes to you and proclaims that Jenkins is out and Circle CI is in! In most organizations around the world this would be a major event. All your pipelines need to be rewritten on Circle CI. It will take months to migrate everything over, not to mention the testing and deployments and, wait a minute! We have everything isolated in Docker containers. This won't be so bad.

We can take the same Docker image we've used in Jenkins and easily run it on another platform. Listing 3-13 shows what the same setup may look like in Circle CI.

Listing 3-13. Running the Docker Container in Circle CI

```
version: 2
jobs:
  build:
    docker:
      - image: YOUR-DOCKER-REGISTRY/YOUR-CUSTOM-IMAGE
    steps:
      - setup_remote_docker:
          docker_layer_caching: true
      - run:
          name: Clone
          command: /stages/01_clone.sh
      - run:
          name: Build
          command: /stages/02_build.sh
      - run:
          name: Test
          command: /stages/03_test.sh
```

```
  - run:
      name: Archive
      command: /stages/04_archive.sh
```

At this point the beauty of the pattern should be clear. While we are just looking at configuration files, you should readily see the similarities. On either platform, we use our Docker image as the basis for running the pipeline. Stages or Steps are defined and given names, like Clone, Build, Test, etc. Next, a Shell script is executed in each section. Since everything runs inside a container, there are no surprises when we execute the pipeline. It will run the same on each platform!

Note   At this point you may be thinking this is way too easy. While this pattern makes moving the code and executing it on another platform crazy easy, you still need to keep in mind the other aspects of running a CI/CD platform. Each will have its own ways of being configured, dealing with networking, etc. However, not having to worry about how to port a pipeline will provide a lot of breathing room if you need to make a switch.

To further illustrate the point of being agnostic, let's look at what this pipeline looks like on another platform. Listing 3-14 shows what the same setup may look like in Travis CI.

Listing 3-14. Running the Docker Container in Travis CI

```
services:
  - docker
before_script:
  - |
    docker run -it -d \
      -v /var/run/docker.sock:/var/run/docker.sock \
      -e DOCKER_USERNAME=${DOCKER_USERNAME} \
```

```
    -e DOCKER_PASSWORD=${DOCKER_PASSWORD} \
    -e GITHUB_URL=${GITHUB_URL} \
    --name MY-PIPELINE \
    YOUR-DOCKER-REGISTRY/YOUR-CUSTOM-IMAGE
script:
  - docker exec MY-PIPELINE /stages/01_clone.sh
  - docker exec MY-PIPELINE /stages/02_build.sh
  - docker exec MY-PIPELINE /stages/03_test.sh
  - docker exec MY-PIPELINE /stages/04_archive.sh
```

In later chapters we'll be using Circle CI and Travis CI to build a very simple pipeline. We'll use the same Docker container and Shell scripts to build, test, and archive an application on both platforms. In fact, the Yaml files shown will be used in those examples!

Overview

We covered a lot of material and patterns in this chapter! Let's take a quick moment to review what we discussed.

Shell Scripts

Shell scripts provide us a way to centralize our pipeline logic into smaller easy to share chunks of code. We can write scripts for very specific functionality and then use them inside "Stage" or "Step" scripts to stitch them together. By doing so, we create scripts that are easier to test and share across multiple pipeline implementations. Also, by using Shell we can be guaranteed they will run across any platform. This pattern also opens us up to using other scripts like Python or PowerShell.

Docker

Docker provides us the isolation needed to simplify the needs of the development team while running on the platform. In the past, the platform would need to have all the runtimes and plugins installed globally for anyone to use. With Docker, the only requirement is that Docker be installed for all to use.

Build Containers

Build containers provide a level of isolation on the platform. Each team can install their own runtimes and dependencies in a container, thus isolating their needs from others. This also provides them with the flexibility to use anything they want, without fear of it affecting the platform. If a team wants to us a bleeding edge release of a runtime, they have the power to do it. They own the build container (or a DevOps team) and are responsible for what goes in it. This allows teams to move at a much more rapid pace than if they were dependent on the platform team.

In the next chapters we'll move out of theory and discussion and into actual implementation. We'll create a simple demo application that we can use to deploy. We'll look at building out our build container and how to implement it in Circle CI and Travis CI. You'll take everything you have learned so far and apply it in a practical way. So let's get started!

CHAPTER 4

A Practical Example

In Chapter 3 we showed you an example of how we can execute a few simulated pipeline stages in a Docker container to create a pipeline that can be ported to any CI server. In this chapter we're going to take it a step further and create a pipeline that can clone, build, test, archive, and deploy a set of working applications. Then, we'll show you how to take the pipeline you've created and move it from your desktop to two popular CI platforms.

An Overview of Our Applications

In this chapter we are focused on applications written using one of three distinct tech stacks; they are:

1. Spring Boot applications written in Java, using Maven as a build automation tool

2. ASP.NET Core Web APIs written in C#

3. Angular applications leveraging TypeScript and Node.js

We've created three sample projects, each using one of these technologies. These projects include everything you need—code, configuration files, Dockerfiles, etc.—to follow along for the rest of the chapter. The next three sections provide a brief overview of what these

B. Atkinson and D. Edwards, *Generic Pipelines Using Docker*,
https://doi.org/10.1007/978-1-4842-3655-0_4

sample applications do and the commands we execute to build, test, and run them. We won't go into detail on how each of the sample applications work—there are other books better suited for that. These are barebones implementations and aren't meant to be used as a model for writing high-quality applications.

Spring Boot

Note   You can find the source code for this project at `https://github.com/Apress/generic-pipelines-using-docker`

The first application is an API written in Java using the Spring Boot framework, and using Maven to build, test, and package the project. It's based off the quick start example on the Spring Boot homepage and works with any relatively recent version of Java and Maven. For the purposes of this book, we're using JDK 8 and Maven 3.

Note   If you want to learn more about the Spring Boot framework and how this project works, check out the quick start guide at `https://projects.spring.io/spring-boot/#quick-start`.

To run the application from the command line, first compile the source code using the `mvn clean package`, then execute `java -jar target/hello.jar`. After a few seconds the application will be up and running. Once it is, open your web browser and navigate to `http://localhost:8080`. You'll receive a simple message: "Hello World!" as shown in Figure 4-1.

Hello World!

Figure 4-1. *The Spring Boot application*

ASP.NET Core Web API

Note   You can find the source code for this project at `https://github.com/Apress/generic-pipelines-using-docker`.

The second application is also an API, but this time written on top of ASP.NET Core Web API. It has a single endpoint that returns an array containing two values. It's based off of the ASP.NET Core Web API project template generated by Visual Studio.

This project uses the commands built into the .NET Core CLI to build and test the project. Using the command line, run `dotnet build ValueApi` to build the project, followed by `dotnet ValueApi/bin/Debug/netcoreapp2.0/ValueApi.dll` to start the API. If you open a browser and navigate to `http://localhost:5000/api/values`, you'll get a response like the one in Figure 4-2.

`["value1","value2"]`

Figure 4-2. *The .NET Core application*

Angular 5

Note   You can find the source code for this project at `https://github.com/Apress/generic-pipelines-using-docker`.

Our last sample project is a web application built using Angular 5, TypeScript, and Node.js and relies on Chromium to run its test suite. It's based on the Angular Quick Start example.

To build and run the project, first download and install the project's dependencies by running `npm install` on the command line. Next, use `npm run build` to compile the project. Finally, host the project in a lightweight web server by running `npm start`. Once the server is running, open a browser and navigate to `http://localhost:4200`. You will see a simple website like the one shown in Figure 4-3.

Welcome to My First Angular App!!

Here are some links to help you start:

- Tour of Heroes
- CLI Documentation
- Angular blog

Figure 4-3.   *The Angular 5 application*

A Deep Dive into the Pipeline

Note   You can find the source code for this project at `https://github.com/Apress/generic-pipelines-using-docker`.

Now that you've got a high-level overview of the sample projects we're dealing with in this chapter, it's time to explore the pipeline itself. In the following sections, we explore the configuration file that drives the behavior of the pipeline. Then we take a close look at each of the five stages of our pipeline: clone, build, test, archive, and deploy. Finally, we take a peek inside the build containers where all this takes place.

The Pipeline Configuration File

Alongside the source code for each application, you'll find a small JSON file named `pipeline.json` that contains some crucial information about the application. The pipeline will use this file to decide everything from how to build the application to where the resulting artifact should be stored for use later. The next three listings show the configuration file for each of our sample projects:

Listing 4-1. The Pipeline Configuration File for the Sample Java Project

```
{
  "application": {
    "name": "Sample Java Application",
    "type": "java"
  },
  "build": {
    "path": null,
    "outputPath": null
  },
```

```
  "test": {
    "enabled": true,
    "path": null
  },
  "archive": {
    "registry": "docker.io",
    "repository": "edwardsdl/sample-java"
  },
  "deploy": {
    "containerPort": 8080
  }
}
```

Listing 4-2. The Pipeline Configuration File for the Sample .NET Core Project

```
{
  "application": {
    "name": "Sample .NET Core App",
    "type": "netcore"
  },
  "build": {
    "path": null,
    "outputPath": "ValueApi/bin/Release/netcoreapp2.0"
  },
  "test": {
    "enabled": true,
    "path": "ValueTests/"
  },
  "archive": {
    "registry": "docker.io",
    "repository": "edwardsdl/sample-netcore"
  },
```

```
  "deploy": {
    "containerPort": 5000
  }
}
```

Listing 4-3. The Pipeline Configuration File for the Sample Node Project

```
{
  "application": {
    "name": "Sample Node App",
    "type": "node"
  },
  "build": {
    "path": null,
    "outputPath": "dist/"
  },
  "test": {
    "enabled": true,
    "path": null
  },
  "archive": {
    "registry": "docker.io",
    "repository": " edwardsdl/sample-node"
  },
  "deploy": {
    "containerPort": 5000
  }
}
```

Our pipeline configuration file is broken into four sections: application, build, test, and archive. Some provide information about the application, while others provide fine-grained control over specific stages in the pipeline. Let's take a closer look at each section.

The application section stores high-level information about the project. We use it to store the name and type of the application. In this book we deal with three types: `node`, `java`, and `netcore`. It's up to you to decide what application types you want to support and what identifiers to assign them. Supporting a greater number of tech stacks will give your developers more flexibility but will require more work on their end. If a new version of the .NET Core framework is released and maintains backwards compatibility, `netcore1`, `netcore2`, and `netcore3` applications can all share a single build image. This is a useful trick for keeping the number of images you have to maintain to a minimum.

The `build` section contains two elements: `path` and `outputPath`. The `path` element is used to let the pipeline know where the applications code can be found when it pulls it from source control. For most projects the source code is located in the root of the repository, but we've found some teams appreciate the flexibility to put it elsewhere. The `outputPath` element lets the pipeline know where to put the compiled output of the build command.

The `test` section contains configuration settings for the test stage of the pipeline. The first property, `enabled`, is used to determine whether this stage is run at all. As your pipeline becomes more robust with additional stages and features, you'll likely find yourself adding this property to other sections too. It can be very useful to turn portions of the pipeline on and off due to unusual situations or for nonstandard projects. The `path` property in this section tells the pipeline where the tests are located relative to the project's root directory.

Caution   If the `enabled` property is setting off alarm bells, that's a good thing! This is useful for teams who don't *yet* have unit tests or need to *temporarily* disable the stage while working through an issue. This has the potential to be used as a crutch!

The archive section lets the pipeline know where the build artifacts—in our case the Docker image containing one of our sample applications—should be stored. The registry property indicates which Docker registry will store the image. In this case, we'll be storing the image on Docker Hub (Docker's public registry). If your organization is hosting their own internal registry, you'd put that here instead. The repository property is the name of the image and should not include any tags; the pipeline will handle all of the tagging automatically. Your organization may require you to store application binaries and images separately. In that case you can modify this section to represent an array of artifact repositories.

The Clone Stage

Typically, the first step in any pipeline is to download a copy of a project's source, and this pipeline is no different. If you haven't already, this would be a good time to clone or review the GitHub examples for the book. In the stages directory, you'll find a file named 01_clone.sh with the following code:

Listing 4-4. The Clone Stage Shell Script

```
#!/usr/bin/env bash

echo
echo "Cloning Application"

git clone "${GITHUB_URL:?}" .
```

There's not much happening in this stage. The script starts by outputting a brief description of the stage and then performing a git clone, which will place the application's source code in the current working directory. Notice we're using an environment variable here—GITHUB_URL. This—and others like it in subsequent stages—are expected to exist wherever the pipeline is running. Stages will also source information from the pipeline.json file. You'll see an example of this in the next stage. We'll cover the pipeline.json file in detail later in this chapter.

The Build Stage

In the second stage the pipeline will build the application. Each tech stack will be handled differently, but the end goal is the same: to create an artifact we can deploy inside a container. In the stages directory, you'll find a file named 02_build.sh with the following code:

Listing 4-5. The Netcore Build Stage Shell Script

```bash
#!/usr/bin/env bash

echo
echo "Building Application"

application_type=$(jq -r .application.type pipeline.json)

case "${application_type}" in
  "java")
    mvn clean package
    ;;
  "netcore")
    dotnet restore
    dotnet build -c Release
    ;;
  "node")
    npm install
    ;;
  *)
```

```
        echo "Unable to build application type ${application_type}"
        exit 1
        ;;
esac
```

This script uses jq to pull the value of application.type out of the pipeline.json file and assign it to application_type. This *should* be set to either java, netcore, or node if the pipline.json file is configured correctly. If application_type doesn't equal one of these values, the script terminates with exit code 1.

Note   jq is a fantastic tool that's packed with functionality! You can find a great tutorial on the official website at https://stedolan.github.io/jq/.

For java applications, we'll use Maven to clean the workspace, which ensures there aren't any cached or outdated files lying around, and then compile the application. It's important to remember that we require all java apps that come through the pipeline to support Maven.

If the application_type is netcore, we'll use the .NET Core CLI to perform a NuGet package restore by issuing the command dotnet restore app. Then, we'll call dotnet build app -c Release to compile the source code using the Release configuration.

Finally, if application_type is set to node, we'll use the Node Package Manager to download and install any required dependencies. After that, we issue the npm run build command to compile everything.

The Test Stage

The third stage of the pipeline handles test execution. You can find it in
03_test.sh.

Listing 4-6. The Test Stage Shell Script

```bash
#!/usr/bin/env bash

echo
echo "Testing Application"

application_type=$(jq -r .application.type pipeline.json)
enabled=$(jq -r .test.enabled pipeline.json)
test_path=$(jq -r .test.path pipeline.json)

if "${enabled}"
then
  echo "Skipped"
  exit 0
fi

case "${application_type}" in
  "java")
    mvn test
    ;;
  "netcore")
    # The path to the test project must be set until
    # https://github.com/Microsoft/vstest/issues/1129 is
    # resolved.
    dotnet test "${test_path}"
    ;;
  "node")
```

```
    npm run test
    ;;
  *)
    echo "Unable to test application type ${application_type}"
    exit 1
    ;;
esac
```

The test stage uses the same pattern as our build stage, with one exception. Before kicking off any tests, it checks the `test.enabled` property in the pipeline configuration file. If it's set to `false`, the stage is skipped.

Assuming the stage is enabled in the configuration file, `application_type` is evaluated and the appropriate command is executed to run the test suite. As in the build stage, unknown application types cause the stage to fail with error code 1.

Using our sample projects, implementing this stage turns out to be fairly trivial. In our experience though, it tends to grow in complexity and even spawn completely new stages. For example, your organization may want to report on code coverage or require a certain percentage of tests to pass. Perhaps your teams have various suites of tests in several different repositories. If your teams write both unit tests and end-to-end tests, it might make sense to keep them in separate stages.

The Archive Stage

Now that the project has been built and tested successfully, it's time to package it into an artifact and place it somewhere safe. In your organization this might be Artifactory, Nexus, GitHub, or any number of other repositories. For our sample projects, we are using Docker Hub. If you're unfamiliar with it, Docker Hub is simply a free, public repository where anyone can store Docker images. The archive stage can be found in `05_archive.sh`.

Listing 4-7. The Archive Stage Shell Script

```bash
#!/usr/bin/env bash

echo
echo "Archiving Application"

registry=$(jq -r .archive.registry pipeline.json)
repository=$(jq -r .archive.repository pipeline.json)
image="${registry}/${repository}:latest"

docker login \
    -u "${DOCKER_USERNAME?:}" \
    -p "${DOCKER_PASSWORD?:}" \
    "${registry}"
docker build -t "${image}" .
docker push "${image}"
```

Like the build and test stages, the archive stage starts off by pulling some information out of the pipeline configuration file. We get the registry and repository values and then combine them to get the desired name of the image containing the application. For now, we're just applying the latest tag, but in the next chapter we'll discuss versioning your artifacts so they won't be overwritten and can be uniquely identified later.

Now that we have a name, we can build and push the image. The first step is to log in to the registry specified in the pipeline configuration file. Like GITHUB_URL, the DOCKER_USERNAME and DOCKER_PASSWORD variables will be passed into the container as environment variables. Because these are credentials and thus sensitive information, they shouldn't be stored in the pipeline configuration file.

Assuming we were able to login successfully, the next step is to build the image. Like we mentioned earlier, each of our sample applications is designed to be deployed inside a container, so each of them has an associated Dockerfile. Our pipeline expects each application's Dockerfile to be located in the project's root directory. Of course, you could always offer more flexibility by introducing a new docker.dockerfilePath variable in your pipeline configuration file. In our experience, however, that hasn't proved to be necessary. To kick off the build, we issue the docker build command passing the name of the image and the build context.

The Deploy Stage

Finally, we reach the deploy stage. There are far too many deployment targets to cover here; every organization is different. For the purposes of this book, 05_deploy.sh will "deploy" to your local machine by simply running the newly created image.

Listing 4-8. The Deploy Stage Shell Script

```
#!/usr/bin/env bash

echo
echo "Deploying Application"

container_port=$(jq -r .deploy.containerPort pipeline.json)
registry=$(jq -r .archive.registry pipeline.json)
repository=$(jq -r .archive.repository pipeline.json)
image="${registry}/${repository}:latest"

docker run -dp "${container_port}:${container_port}" "${image}"
```

As mentioned before, each of our example apps are designed to be deployed inside a container. To do that, we need a few pieces of information from the pipeline configuration file: archive.registry, archive.namespace, and archive.repository. We put these together to form an image name, for example, docker.io/edwardsdl/sample-netcore:latest. This is the image we created in the archive phase.

Next, we execute the command `docker run -dp "${container_port}:${container_port}" "${image}"`. This runs the latest version of the image containing our application in "detached" mode—meaning in the background—and publishes the port the application is listening on. Once this is done, the deploy script terminates, which, since it is the last of the stage scripts, causes the pipeline container to exit.

Tip While containerizing your applications isn't necessary to create a generic pipeline, it certainly makes things easier. If your organization hasn't explored the idea of containerized applications, I *highly* recommend doing so.

A Look at Our Build Containers

One of the key features of our pipeline is that it executes entirely inside a Docker container. This allows us total control over our build environment. We can add or update dependencies easily, set environment variables as needed, or install software in custom locations—all without interfering with other applications' build environments or workflows. Of course, in order to have a build container you must have a Dockerfile. In this section we'll take a look at the three Dockerfiles we use for each of our three tech stacks.

First let's look inside `Dockerfile.java`. As you may have guessed, this is the Dockerfile we use to construct the image for our Java build containers.

Listing 4-9. The Dockerfile for the Java Build Container

```
FROM maven:3-jdk-8

RUN curl -fsSL get.docker.com | sh

RUN apt-get update && apt-get install -y jq zip
```

```
COPY stages stages

WORKDIR /app
```

The Dockerfile is relatively simple. We use maven:3-jdk-8 as our base image because it comes out of the box with both the Java 8 JDK and Maven 3. Admittedly this base image makes the container a little bloated, but in our experience these containers tend to get fairly large anyway, so it's not worth worrying about a few extra megabytes.

Next, we install Docker inside the container. That probably sounds strange—it did to us the first time too! The reason is simple: our applications are designed to be deployed *as containers* and thus have Dockerfiles themselves. That means we need to issue docker build and docker push commands from *inside* our build containers.

Caution   We chose to install Docker using this method because it's concise and easy to understand. However, it's never a good idea to run scripts without examining them first. You can find a more secure method for installing Docker at https://docs.docker.com/install/.

Note   Using Docker inside of Docker is becoming a very common scenario. However, if you are new to this concept you can learn more here: https://blog.docker.com/2013/09/docker-can-now-run-within-docker/.

The third line of our Dockerfile installs two packages: jq and zip. The first, jq, is a command line tool that's great for parsing and transforming JSON data. It's used extensively inside our stage scripts, as you saw earlier in the chapter. The second is zip. I'm sure you can guess what that does.

Next, we copy the pipeline stages into the container. Be aware: by copying your code in now, you'll be required to recreate your build images when your stage scripts change. In your implementation you may decide to clone your stages into your container when it starts up. You'll always be running the latest code, but it's more difficult to determine which version of the pipeline created a given artifact.

Finally, we set our working directory to /app. The pipeline will use this as its primary workspace. Application code will be cloned, built, tested, and packaged all within this directory.

We use Dockerfile.netcore to create the build container for .NET Core projects, which looks very similar to its Spring Boot counterpart. In this case we use microsoft/netcore:2-sdk as our base image instead of maven:3-jdk-8. Otherwise, this file is exactly the same.

Listing 4-10. The Dockerfile for the .NET Core Pipeline Image

```
FROM microsoft/dotnet:2-sdk

RUN curl -fsSL get.docker.com | sh

RUN apt-get update && apt-get install -y jq zip

COPY stages stages

WORKDIR /app
```

The Dockerfile for the Angular tech stack follows the same pattern as the previous two. In this case our base image will be node:9-stretch, which uses a recent version of Debian Linux and provides easy access to Node.js and NPM. We also install two additional dependencies: chromium and chromium-driver. These are used by our application's test suite. We've named this file Dockerfile.node.

Listing 4-11. The Dockerfile for the Angular Pipeline Image

```
FROM node:9-stretch

RUN curl -fsSL get.docker.com | sh

RUN apt-get update && apt-get install -y \
    chromium \
    chromium-driver \
    jq \
    zip

COPY stages stages

WORKDIR /app
```

Running the Pipeline

Now that we've gone over the sample applications, stage scripts, and Dockerfiles, it's time to run our pipeline. To begin, we'll run it locally. Afterwards we'll show you how to port it to several popular CI tools.

Before you move on, we suggest you fork one of our sample projects. These applications have been thoroughly tested, and with a few simple modifications you'll be able to run them through the pipeline locally *and* in the cloud. In addition, as part of the sign-up process, both Travis CI and CircleCI will request access to your GitHub account in order to streamline the setup process and start builds when new code is committed to a linked repository. In the end, we think it'll be easier for you to use one of our applications than build your own.

For the rest of the chapter we'll be using our sample .NET Core project. You can find it at https://github.com/Apress/generic-pipelines-using-docker. If you're using GitHub, forking our sample projects is easy! Just navigate to its repository on GitHub and click the "Fork" button in the top right. This will create a copy of the repository in your account.

Using the Command Line

Running the pipeline from the command line is pretty straightforward. First you build the Docker image for the pipeline you want to use by issuing the docker build command. Next you run the image passing along all of the required arguments to mount the Docker socket and set the appropriate environment variables. For example, if you want to build the sample .NET Core app, you'd issue the following commands from the root of the directory containing your application:

Listing 4-12. Building and Running the Pipeline

```
docker build -t pipeline -f <Dockerfile> .

docker run \
  -v /var/run/docker.sock:/var/run/docker.sock \
  --env GITHUB_URL=https://github.com/edwardsdl/sample-netcore.
  git \
  --env DOCKER_USERNAME=AzureDiamond \
  --env DOCKER_PASSWORD=hunter2 \
  pipeline \
  /stages/00_run.sh
```

Obviously, the values for GITHUB_URL, DOCKER_USERNAME, and DOCKER_ PASSWORD are placeholders. You need to replace them with the path for your fork and your Docker Hub credentials. Remember to use your Docker repository URL as well! Once you've run the docker run command, you'll see the pipeline go through each of the stages we described earlier. Your output should look like that in Figure 4-4.

```
Cloning Application
Cloning into '.'...

Building Application
  Restoring packages for /app/ValueTests/ValueTests.csproj...
  Restoring packages for /app/ValueTests/ValueTests.csproj...
  Restoring packages for /app/ValueApi/ValueApi.csproj...
  Restoring packages for /app/ValueApi/ValueApi.csproj...
  Installing Microsoft.VisualStudio.Web.CodeGeneration.Contracts 2.0.1.
  Installing Microsoft.VisualStudio.Web.CodeGeneration.Tools 2.0.1.
  Restore completed in 1.34 sec for /app/ValueApi/ValueApi.csproj.
  Installing Microsoft.AspNetCore.SpaServices 2.0.1.
  Installing Microsoft.AspNetCore.NodeServices 2.0.1.
  Installing Microsoft.AspNetCore.Mvc.Core 2.0.1.
  Installing Microsoft.AspNetCore.Mvc.RazorPages 2.0.1.
  Installing Microsoft.AspNetCore.Mvc.ViewFeatures 2.0.1.
  Installing Microsoft.AspNetCore.Mvc.All 2.0.3.
  Installing Microsoft.AspNetCore.Mvc.Cors 2.0.1.
  Installing Microsoft.AspNetCore.Mvc.Razor 2.0.1.
  Installing Microsoft.AspNetCore.Mvc.DataAnnotations 2.0.1.
  Installing Microsoft.AspNetCore.Mvc 2.0.1.
  Installing Microsoft.AspNetCore.Mvc.Abstractions 2.0.1.
  Installing Microsoft.AspNetCore.Mvc.ApiExplorer 2.0.1.
```

Figure 4-4. *Running the pipeline from the command line*

In its final stage, the pipeline will "deploy" the sample .NET Core application locally. When you issue the docker ps command as in Figure 4-5, you'll see you have one container running—the one running the sample application! Using your browser, navigate to http://localhost:5000/api/values to verify it's working.

```
$ docker ps
CONTAINER ID        IMAGE                                   COMMAND
ba88f237dc0d        edwardsdl/sample-netcore:latest         "dotnet /app/ValueAp…"
$ ▮
```

Figure 4-5. *Inspecting the deployed application*

Using IntelliJ IDEA CE

If you're more comfortable using an IDE, Intellij IDEA has wonderful support for building Docker images. You can use the "Docker Integration" plugin, which is incredibly helpful. Setup is a little more involved, but once you're done you have a powerful development environment at your fingertips.

Tip   If you run into trouble when adding new Docker configuration profiles, check out JetBrains' help page at www.jetbrains.com/ help/idea/run-debug-configuration-docker.html.

To begin, we will create a few new configurations in our IDE. In the top right corner, click the "Select Run/Debug Configuration" drop-down box and click "Edit Configurations…" as in Figure 4-6.

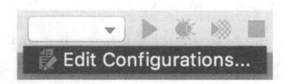

Figure 4-6.   *Creating a new configuration*

On the Run/Debug Configuration window, create a new Docker configuration by clicking on the "Add New Configuration" button in the top left. Under the "Docker" menu item, select "Dockerfile" as shown in Figure 4-7.

Add New Configuration		
⌶ Android JUnit		Click the + button to
☀ Ant Target	ests	
▣ Applet		
⬚ Application		
▮ Compound		
🂠 Docker ▸	Add New 'Docker' Configuration	
◉ Gradle	🂠 Docker Image	
⊚ Griffon	🂠 Docker-compose	
▊ JAR Application	🂠 Dockerfile	

Figure 4-7.   *Adding a new Dockerfile configuration*

The first configuration we'll create will allow us to run the .NET Core pipeline. We'll name this new configuration, "Run .NET Core Pipeline." In the Dockerfile drop-down box, select "Dockerfile.netcore." Now, select the checkbox labelled "Run built image" and set the container name to `netcore-pipeline`. Next, in the executable section, set the command to `/stages/00_run.sh`.

Now we need to mount the host's Docker socket inside the container. This is what makes it possible for us to execute Docker commands *inside* the container. To do this, click the button labelled, "..." to the right of the bind mounts textbox. In the "Bind Mounts" window, add a new bind mount setting both the host path and the container path to `/var/run/docker.sock` (Figure 4-8).

Host path	Container path	Read only
/var/run/docker.sock	/var/run/docker.sock	☐

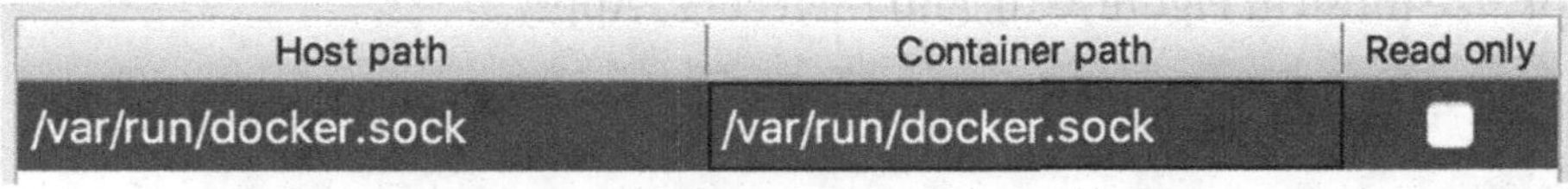

Figure 4-8. *Mounting the Docker socket*

Tip   If you want to learn more about the history of issuing Docker commands inside a container and mounting the Docker socket, Jérôme Petazzoni has written an excellent blog post at `https://jpetazzo.github.io/2015/09/03/do-not-use-docker-in-docker-for-ci/`.

Next, we'll need to add a few environment variables (Figure 4-9), specifically `GITHUB_URL`, `DOCKER_USERNAME`, and `DOCKER_PASSWORD`. The value of `GITHUB_URL` will be `DOCKER_PASSWORD` will be your Docker Hub username and password, respectively. The values we use here are placeholders and won't work for you.es we use here are placeholders and won't work for you.

Name	Value
GITHUB_URL	https://github.com/edwardsdl/sa...
DOCKER_USERNAME	AzureDiamond
DOCKER_PASSWORD	hunter2

Figure 4-9. *Adding environment variables*

Note   If you have forked the sample GitHub repo, remember to use your GITHUB_URL in these examples!

After you've added the environment variables, click the OK button to return to the Run/Debug Configurations screen. Confirm that your settings look like those in Figure 4-10, and then click "Apply."

Name:	Run .NET Core Pipeline	Share Single instance only
Server:	🠻 Docker	⬍ ...
Dockerfile:	Dockerfile.netcore	⌄ ...
Image tag:	netcore-pipeline	
Build args:		...
☑ Run built image		
Container name:	netcore-pipeline	
Executable		
Entrypoint:		
Command:	/stages/00_run.sh	
Publish exposed ports to the host interfaces:	○ All ● Specify	
Bind ports:		...
Bind mounts:	/var/run/docker.sock:/var/run/docker.sock	...
Environment variables:	it; DOCKER_USERNAME=AzureDiamond; DOCKER_PASSWORD=hunter2	...
Command line options:		
Command preview:	-name netcore-pipeline netcore-pipeline /stages/00_run.sh	

Figure 4-10. *Adding the Run .NET Core Pipeline configuration*

Next, we'll repeat this process to create additional configuration profiles for our Java and Node pipelines. Most of the process is identical, but you'll want to be sure to choose the correct Dockerfile and GITHUB_URL values. Reference Figures 4-11 and 4-12 to ensure your settings are correct.

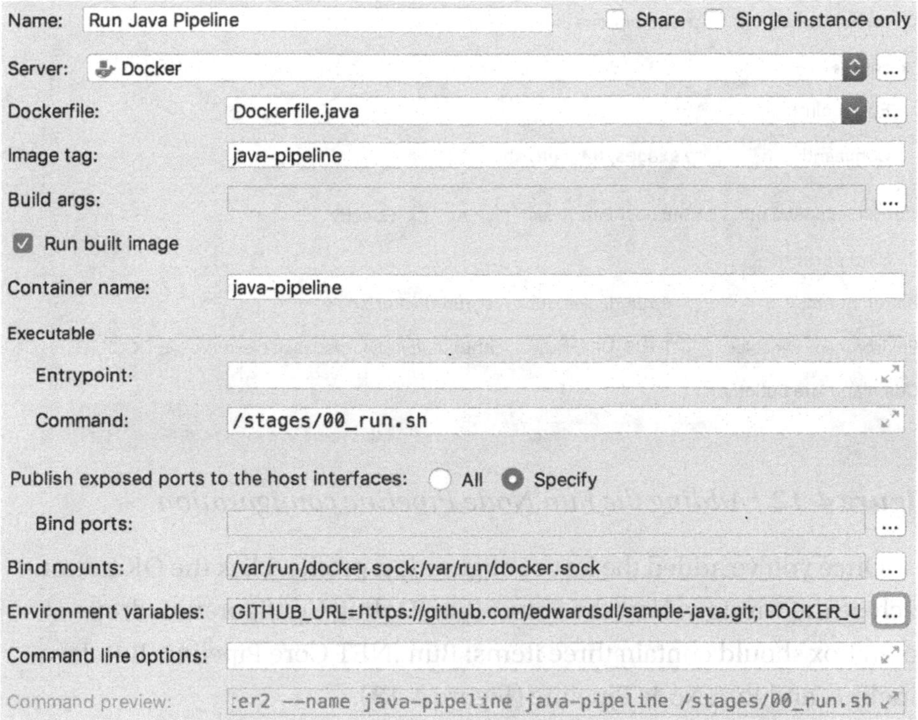

Figure 4-11. *Adding the Run Java Pipeline configuration*

Name:	Run Node Pipeline		Share	Single instance only

Server:	🐳 Docker
Dockerfile:	Dockerfile.node
Image tag:	node-pipeline
Build args:	
☑ Run built image	
Container name:	node-pipeline

Executable

Entrypoint:	
Command:	/stages/00_run.sh

Publish exposed ports to the host interfaces: ○ All ● Specify

Bind ports:	
Bind mounts:	/var/run/docker.sock:/var/run/docker.sock
Environment variables:	GITHUB_URL=https://github.com/edwardsdl/sample-node.git; DOCKER_
Command line options:	
Command preview:	:er2 --name node-pipeline node-pipeline /stages/00_run.sh

Figure 4-12. *Adding the Run Node Pipeline configuration*

Once you've added the last configuration profile, click the OK button
to close the window. Now the Select Run/Debug Configuration drop-
down box should contain three items: Run .NET Core Pipeline, Run Java
Pipeline, and Run Node Pipeline (Figure 4-13).

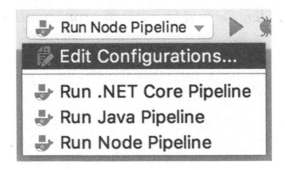

Figure 4-13. *Listing the newly created configuration profiles*

Moving to the Cloud

Now that we've seen the pipeline work on our local machine, it's time to get it working using a real continuous integration tool. We'll start by forking one of our sample projects in GitHub. Next, we'll show you how to run our pipeline in Travis CI by converting the 00_run.sh script to a .travis.yml file. Finally, we'll walk you through porting our pipeline from Travis CI to CircleCI.

Moving the Pipeline to Travis CI

As mentioned, we'll be showing you how to use the pipeline with two continuous integration platforms. Up first, we'll be looking at Travis CI.

Travis CI was one of the first—if not *the* first—CI/CD SaaS offering. It provides an intuitive interface, free accounts for open source projects, good documentation, and a large number of integrations. Because of this, Travis CI is wildly popular, especially amongst open source projects.

Creating a Travis CI Account

Before we can move our pipeline to Travis CI, we'll need to create a new account. If you don't need help, skip ahead to the next section.

Open a browser and navigate to https://travis-ci.org, then click the button labeled, "Sign Up" (Figure 4-14). If prompted, enter your GitHub username and password. If you are already signed in to GitHub, you won't be asked to do so again.

Caution   Check that top-level domain! You want https://travis-ci.org **not** https://travis-ci.com. The latter is for paid projects only!

Figure 4-14. *The Travis CI homepage*

Grant Travis CI access to your email address and permission to add new webhooks to your repositories. The service will use this to help you set up new builds, to trigger builds when new code is committed to your repositories, and notify you when things go wrong.

After granting Travis CI access, you'll be dropped on a "Getting Started" page. Take a minute to read through this page. It details the steps required to add a new repository and start building it.

Adding a New Repository

Now that your account has been created, you're ready to add a new repository to Travis CI. This is where it all comes together. Once you're done setting up the repository, you'll get to see the generic pipeline in action.

Head to your profile page by using the link in the instructions. Alternatively, you can click the "Profile" link in the drop-down menu located in the top right of the navigation bar, as shown in Figure 4-15.

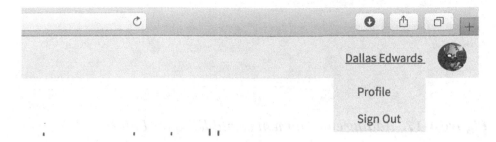

Figure 4-15. *The "Getting Started" page*

On your profile page, search for "sample." This will return a list of any of our sample projects you forked. Click the gray toggle switch to the left of "sample-netcore" to allow Travis CI to integrate with the repository (Figure 4-16).

Legacy Services Integration

sample	

sample-java	Settings
sample-node	Settings
sample-netcore	Settings

Figure 4-16. *Adding the .NET Core sample repository to Travis CI*

Now click on the "Settings" button to the right of the toggle switch to navigate to the settings for this repository. Before we start the first build, we need to tell Travis CI what environment variables to pass to our container (Figure 4-17). These will be the same values you used when running the pipeline locally: DOCKER_USERNAME, DOCKER_PASSWORD, and GITHUB_URL.

Environment Variables

Notice that the values are not escaped when your builds are executed. Special characters (for bash) should be escaped accordingly.

DOCKER_PASSWORD   ●●●●●●●●●●●●●●●●   🗑

DOCKER_USERNAME   AzureDiamond   🗑

GITHUB_URL   https://github.com/edwardsdl/sample   🗑

Figure 4-17. *Adding environment variables to the build*

Caution   Make sure to toggle the "Display value in build log" switch to the OFF position for the DOCKER_PASSWORD environment variable. You don't want your password showing up in the build log!

Now everything is ready for us to kick off our first build! Click the "More options" button on the top right side of the page and select "Trigger build" from the drop-down menu (Figure 4-18).

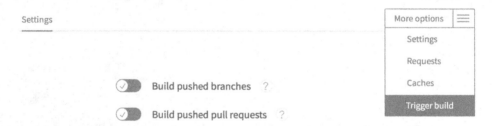

Figure 4-18. *Triggering the first build*

You'll be prompted to select a branch and add a custom commit message and custom configuration. Essentially Travis CI is *simulating* a commit to your Git repository; nothing is actually pushed. This is actually an incredibly useful feature, especially when you're getting started! It allows you to quickly test changes to your configuration file without having to go through the *change, commit, push* loop over and over again. For now, just click the "Trigger custom build" button at the bottom (Figure 4-19).

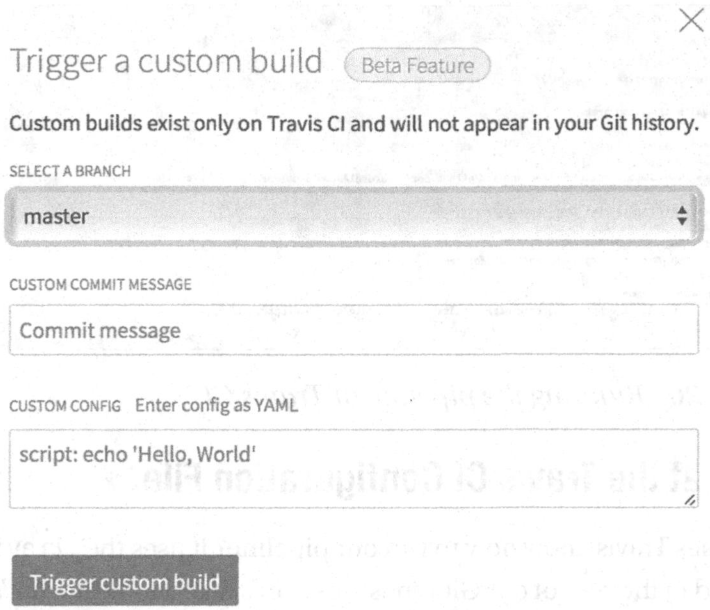

Trigger a custom build   (Beta Feature)

Custom builds exist only on Travis CI and will not appear in your Git history.

SELECT A BRANCH

```
master
```

CUSTOM COMMIT MESSAGE

```
Commit message
```

CUSTOM CONFIG   Enter config as YAML

```
script: echo 'Hello, World'
```

Trigger custom build

Figure 4-19. *Triggering a custom build*

Note   For more information about this feature, check out the blog post announcing its release at `https://blog.travis-ci.com/2017-08-24-trigger-custom-build`.

You'll be redirected to a page showing you a detailed, real-time status of your first build (Figure 4-20). If you scroll through the logs at the bottom, you'll notice some familiar messages! The application is being cloned, built, tested, and archived just like it was when you ran the pipeline locally!

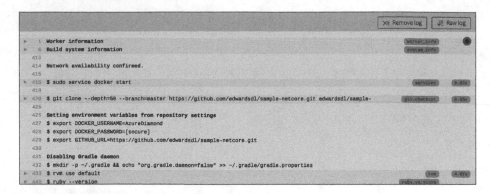

Figure 4-20. *Running the pipeline in Travis CI*

A Look at the Travis CI Configuration File

So how does Travis know how to run our pipeline? It uses the `.travis.yml`
file located in the root of our Git repository. Let's take a look at what's inside!

Listing 4-13. The Travis CI Configuration File

```
services:
  - docker
before_script:
  - |
    docker run -it -d \
      -v /var/run/docker.sock:/var/run/docker.sock \
      -e DOCKER_USERNAME=${DOCKER_USERNAME} \
      -e DOCKER_PASSWORD=${DOCKER_PASSWORD} \
      -e GITHUB_URL=${GITHUB_URL} \
      --name netcore-pipeline \
      edwardsdl/netcore-pipeline:latest
script:
  - docker exec netcore-pipeline /stages/01_clone.sh
  - docker exec netcore-pipeline /stages/02_build.sh
  - docker exec netcore-pipeline /stages/03_test.sh
  - docker exec netcore-pipeline /stages/04_archive.sh
```

It turns out the configuration file looks pretty similar to our `00_run.sh` script. That's by design! One of the primary benefits of this architecture is the ease with which you can move from one CI platform to another.

The `services` section describes any custom services—like MongoDB, Memcached, or RabbitMQ—your build requires. Travis CI will include these in your build environment. In our case, we ask that Docker be installed.

The `before_script` section lets us run any last-minute commands before the build *really* gets started. We'll use it to pull and run the latest version of the `netcore-pipeline` Docker image. Just like when we ran it locally, we mount the Docker socket and pass the `DOCKER_USERNAME`, `DOCKER_PASSWORD`, and `GITHUB_URL` environment variables to the container.

Note   You may have noticed our `docker run` command is preceded by a vertical bar (`|`). This is called the *literal block scalar style* and it allows our command to span multiple lines. If you're fascinated by formal language grammars, check out the YAML specification at `http://yaml.org/spec/1.2/spec.html#id2795688`.

The `script` section is where we instruct Travis CI to run the stages we've included inside the container. Starting at `01_clone.sh`, we simply work our way through each script until we're done. If any stage fails, Travis will stop execution and mark the build as failing.

Note   For more information about configuring your Travis CI build, visit `https://docs.travis-ci.com/user/customizing-the-build/`.

Running the Pipeline in CircleCI

It's not unusual for organizations to transition from one CI/CD platform to another. Even upgrading from one version to another can be a huge undertaking. In this section, we'll see what it takes to move our pipeline from Travis CI to CircleCI.

CircleCI is one of the world's most popular CI/CD platforms. Like Travis CI, CircleCI is hosted in the cloud, offers free accounts, and is *very* easy to get up and running. On top of all that, it's arguably an even better fit for our pipeline than Travis CI, as it was built with containerized pipelines in mind!

Creating a CircleCI Account

Tip   For more information about getting started with CircleCI, visit the 2.0 documentation page at `https://circleci.com/docs/2.0/`.

This section will guide you through the process of creating an account. The process is fairly straightforward and very similar to that of Travis CI. If you've got experience working with CircleCI or are confident you don't need help, feel free to skip to the next section.

To begin, open a browser and navigate to `https://circleci.com`. In the top right corner, click the button labelled "Sign Up" (Figure 4-21).

Figure 4-21. The CircleCI home page

CircleCI will ask you to decide whether you want to sign up using
GitHub or BitBucket (Figure 4-22). We'll be using GitHub; but if you want
to use BitBucket, it should be easy to follow along, as the process is almost
identical.

Figure 4-22. *Signing up with CircleCI*

If prompted, enter your GitHub username and password (Figure 4-23).
If you are already signed in to GitHub, you won't be asked to do so again.

Figure 4-23. *Signing up using GitHub*

97

Next, CircleCI will request access to your email address and read access to your repositories (Figure 4-24). Like Travis CI, this information will be used to help set up your projects and notify you when your builds break.

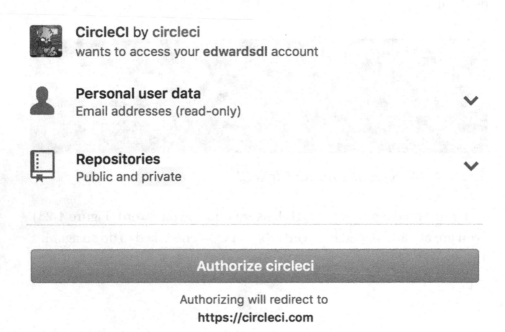

Figure 4-24. *Authorizing CircleCI to access GitHub repositories*

Creating a New CircleCI Project

After creating your account, you'll be sent to your dashboard. This is where you'll go to view the latest information on all your builds. At the moment, however, you have no projects. Instead of build information, you'll be presented with a page welcoming you to the platform and directing you to add a new project (Figure 4-25). That sounds like a great idea!

Figure 4-25. *The builds screen*

To begin, click the blue "Add projects" button in the center of the page. This will take you to a list of all the repositories in your GitHub or BitBucket account.

In the list of repositories, find the fork you created of the sample .NET Core repository and click the "Set Up Project" button (Figure 4-26).

Figure 4-26. *Adding a new project*

Tip   Make sure the "Show Forks" checkbox is selected, otherwise your repository won't show up in the list.

On the Add Project screen, select Linux as the operating system and choose "Other" under the Language section (Figure 4-27). Out of the box, CircleCI comes with the ability to intelligently build and test projects written using some popular technologies. While this is a wonderful feature, we won't be using it for this or any of our other sample applications. All of our projects include a configuration file that tells CircleCI exactly what to commands to execute. We'll take a closer look at this file a little later.

Operating System

| ⚲ Linux | 🍎 macOS |

Language

| ⚙ Clojure | ⚙ Elixir | ⚙ Go | ⚙ Gradle (Java) | ⚙ Maven (Java) | ⚙ Node | ⚙ PHP | ⚙ Python | ⚙ Ruby |
| ⚙ Scala | ⚙ Other |

Next Steps

You're almost there! We're going to walk you through setting up a configuration file, committing it, and turning on our listener so that CircleCI can test your commits.

Want to skip ahead? Jump right into our documentation, set up a .yml file, and kick off your build with the button below.

| 1. | Create a folder named `.circleci` and add a file `config.yml` (so that the filepath be in `.circleci/config.yml`). | |
| 2. | Populate the config.yml with the contents of the sample .yml (shown below). | Copy To Clipboard |

Figure 4-27. *Setting up the sample .NET Core project*

After configuring the project, click the "Start building" button to create the CircleCI project and start a build.

Once you've started the build, you'll be taken to a new page showing you its status (Figure 4-28). The build starts by pulling down our pipeline image, in this case `edwardsdl/netcore-pipeline:latest`, and then it begins executing the instructions found in the sample project's `config.yml` file. Almost immediately however, the build fails! Checking the output of the Clone section makes the problem obvious: `stages/01_clone.sh: line 6: GITHUB_URL: parameter null or not set`. We never set the `GITHUB_URL` environment variable!

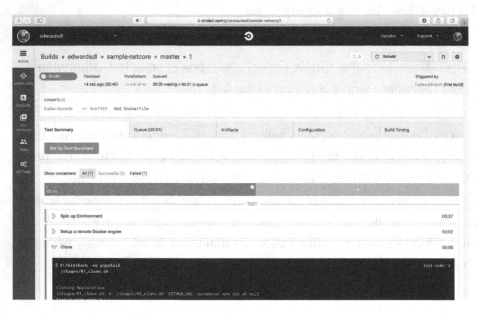

Figure 4-28. *The first build of the sample .NET Core project*

To fix this, you'll need to navigate to the build settings for the project and set a few environment variables (Figure 4-29). Go to the settings page by clicking the button with the gear shaped icon at the top right. Then click the "Environment Variables" link under the "Build Settings" section (Figure 4-30). Next use the "Add Variable" button to add three new environment variables: GITHUB_URL, DOCKER_USERNAME, and DOCKER_PASSWORD. Unlike Travis CI, the values you set here cannot be exposed in plain text.

Figure 4-29. *Projects page in Circle CI*

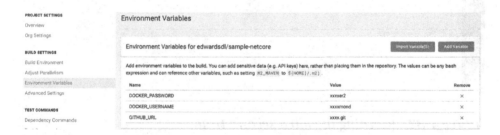

Figure 4-30. *Adding environment variables*

Now that we've set our environment variables, go back to the list of builds by clicking the "Builds" button at the top of the navigation bar on the left side. You should see a single row giving a summary of our failed build (Figure 4-31). Find the "rebuild" link on this row and click it.

Figure 4-31. *Rebuilding the project*

After you click the "rebuild" link, you'll be taken back to the
build details page (Figure 4-32). This time the build should complete
successfully! If you examine the build actions list, the output should look
familiar. All of our stages are listed, and the output is the same as we saw
when running the pipeline locally!

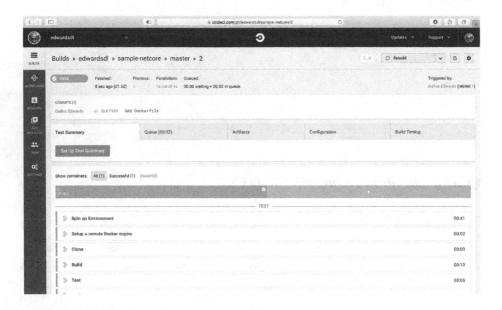

Figure 4-32. *Running the job a second time*

A Look at the CircleCI Configuration File

So how did CircleCI know how to execute our stages? Take a look at one of
our sample projects and you'll find a hidden directory named `.circleci`.
Inside this directory you'll find a single file named `config.yml`. This is the
CircleCI configuration file, and it tells CircleCI everything it needs to know.
In the sample .NET Core app, this YAML file looks like this:

Listing 4-14. The sample-netcore config.yml File

```yaml
version: 2
jobs:
  build:
    docker:
      - image: edwardsdl/netcore-pipeline:latest
    steps:
      - setup_remote_docker:
          docker_layer_caching: true
      - run:
          name: Clone
          command: /stages/01_clone.sh
      - run:
          name: Build
          command: /stages/02_build.sh
      - run:
          name: Test
          command: /stages/03_test.sh
      - run:
          name: Archive
          command: /stages/04_archive.sh
```

The file starts by specifying the Docker image to use when executing the pipeline steps. Those steps are defined in the next section. Most of this should look familiar—the clone stage is run first, followed by the build, test, and archive stages. The setup_remote_docker step is new though. This is what allows us to run Docker commands inside our container.

Note   You can find more information about CircleCI's config.yml file at https://circleci.com/docs/2.0/configuration-reference/.

Overview

In this chapter we took a deep dive into all the components necessary to build a simple, albeit fully functional, generic pipeline. We gave examples of several critical pipeline stages: clone, build, test, archive, and deploy. We then took a look at the Dockerfiles we use to create our build environments.

We then put it all together and used our pipeline to build and deploy several sample applications on our local machines. Taking it one step further, we showed you how easy it is to migrate the pipeline from your local machine to Travis CI and then to CircleCI.

In the next chapter, we cover more advanced topics and show you how to tackle some of the problems that tend to show up in real-world implementations.

CHAPTER 5

Moving Beyond the Basics

We've covered a lot in this book so far. You've seen the transition from monolithic one pipeline per application style CI/CD processes all the way to a fully generic implementation. At this point we've created a truly generic and platform-independent pipeline that can deploy any number of languages expanded upon and even look at implementations in some other scripting languages. The goal of this chapter is to expand on the knowledge gained so far, and to further explore and emphasize the power of generic pipelines.

By the end of this chapter we'll have seen what the generic pipeline may look like in a true enterprise implementation. We'll also look at the role each team plays in its implementation and how a federated DevOps team may come into play. We'll even explore how you can empower your development teams to take control of the pipeline and run custom scripts.

Additional Stages and Steps

So far we've built a somewhat basic pipeline with a minimum number of stages. While this is more than enough to get you up to speed on how to build a generic pipeline, we've only scratched the surface of what

© Brandon Atkinson, Dallas Edwards 2018
B. Atkinson and D. Edwards, *Generic Pipelines Using Docker*,
https://doi.org/10.1007/978-1-4842-3655-0_5

the pipeline would look like in a production environment. Our pipeline consists of the following stages:

- Clone

- Build

- Unit Test

- Deploy

There are many organizations that would be thrilled to simply have a pipeline with these stages. We talked in Chapter 1 about how there are companies, even today, that still deploy code manually. A simple pipeline like the one in this book would be a godsend for them. However, for companies that truly embrace DevOps and automated CI/CD pipelines, this is simply not enough to meet their needs.

A proper enterprise-ready pipeline requires stages that cover much more, including:

- *Static Code Analysis*: This stage would perform code coverage checks and linting on your application source code.

- *Security Scan*: This stage would perform security and vulnerability scanning on the source code. This stage is crucial to ensure the application is secure and not vulnerable to cyberattacks.

- *Licensing Scan*: This stage would perform licensing checks on any third-party code incorporated into the application. Some organizations have strict rules around the licensing of code and may restrict what can be deployed.

- *Artifact Storage*: This stage would take the built application code and store it in a repository for later use. This allows for easy promotion of code that has been built and tested and has passed all the necessary checks before being released to Production.

- *End to End Tests*: This stage would perform any automated tests against the deployed application. This is where you can initiate test suites to test any functionality that is required to go to Production.

- *Performance Tests*: This stage would kick off any performance tests that are needed to exert a load on the application. This could be combined with End to End tests if needed.

That is a total of ten stages including the ones we included in the earlier chapters! As you can see, an enterprise CI/CD pipeline can be quite complex. Each stage may interact with one or more systems, one or more times! It's quite easy to imagine some of these stages making multiple calls to the same system as well. For instance, you may need to submit source code for a security scan, and then make another call to check the results.

We haven't even talked about pipelines that may need to also provision infrastructure as part of their deployments. Some enterprises use the deployment of new code to also create a new server stack in the process. This is common with cloud providers like AWS. If you have an application that runs on EC2 instances, for example, you may want to provision a new instance with a fresh copy of the underlying OS on each deployment. This gives you an opportunity to get the latest security patches on the OS each time you deploy.

The number of stages you have can be limitless. However, the ones listed earlier would be the most commonly used. The main takeaway is that your pipeline may consist of multiple stages and may need to handle multiple languages. The nice part is, outside of the build and unit test stages, most of the remaining stages are generally not language specific. This makes building and testing those much easier.

Again, we must stress that standards are your friends with regard to all your stages. The generic pipeline is built to handle any number of languages passed to it, so your stages must handle those accordingly. If you're using enterprise-grade tools for scanning, this is probably not going to be an issue. For instance, more static code scanning tools can handle pretty much any code language you can throw at it. The goal in the later stages of the pipeline is to continue to enforce standards and further push the generic pattern.

Other Scripting Languages

While shell scripts are very powerful and almost guaranteed to run anywhere, you may find yourself in a situation where you either don't want to use Shell scripts, or can't. One of the benefits of the pattern covered in this book is that it can be applied to any scripting language you wish. In fact, it doesn't even have to be a scripting language! You could accomplish the same goals using any language: for instance, Golang may be a nice option.

We talked at length in the book about why we chose Shell over other languages. Scripting languages are interpreted rather than compiled; this provides many benefits. For instance, using Shell allows us to pretty much run in any Linux environment without issues. Bash would be another excellent choice with the introduction of native Bash in Windows environments. This is what makes scripting languages a great choice for this pattern.

> **Note**   Windows 10 is required for native Bash in Windows. The
> Windows Subsystem for Linux allows you to run Linux environments
> without the overhead of a virtual machine. You can learn more at
> the following link: `https://docs.microsoft.com/en-us/`
> `windows/wsl/about`.

Using a compiled language like Golang or C# is not a horrible choice,
but it introduces additional hurdles. Aside from needing to recompile your
code each time you make a change, it also requires you to install a runtime,
deal with versioning problems, and work around platform specific
issues. If you needed to jump from a Windows environment to a Linux
environment, you would need to compile it separately for each one. If you
were using Bash scripts, you would not need to be bothered; simply pick
up the code and change operating systems.

We've explored Shell scripts in detail. Now let's look at the same
examples but in other languages. We'll basically show each stage we've
seen already but presented in another language.

PowerShell

Listing 5-1 shows the build stage in PowerShell.

Listing 5-1. PowerShell Build Stage Script

```
$application_type = application.type

switch ( $application_type )
{
    java
    {
        mvn clean package
    }
```

```
netcore
{
    dotnet restore
    dotnet build -c Release
}
node
{
    npm install
}
default
{
    Write-Host "Unable to build application type
    $application_type."
    exit 1
}
}
```

This script assumes that you have parsed your JSON configuration file and the application type is accessible via an object. Listing 5-2 shows the test stage script.

Listing 5-2. PowerShell Unit Test Stage Script

```
$application_type = application.type
$test_path = test.path

switch ( $application_type )
{
    java
    {
        mvn test
    }
```

```
netcore
{
    dotnet test $test_path
}
node
{
    npm run test
}
default
{
    Write-Host "Unable to test application type
    $application_type."
    exit 1
}
}
```

You should be noticing a familiar pattern at this point. Even with PowerShell, the same patterns from the Shell scripts are in place. As with the build stage, your JSON configuration file has been parsed and is available to your script. Listing 5-3 illustrates the archive stage.

Listing 5-3. PowerShell Archive Stage Script

```
$registry = archive.registry
$namespace = archive.namespace
$repository = archive.repository
$image = "$registry/$namespace/$repository:latest"

docker login `
    -u $DOCKER_USERNAME `
    -p $DOCKER_PASSWORD `
    $registry
docker build -t $image
docker push $image
```

Finally, listing 5-4 illustrates the deploy stage.

Listing 5-4. PowerShell Deploy Stage Script

```
$registry = archive.registry
$namespace = archive.namespace
$repository = archive.repository
$image = "$registry/$namespace/$repository:latest"
docker run -dP $image
```

What is truly amazing here are the similarities between the Shell script and PowerShell. Even though they are completely different scripting languages, the code looks nearly identical. Again, this is the power of standards coming into play. By keeping your code lean and sticking to the core commands in each language, you will find your scripts are small, lightweight, and ultimately easily transferrable to another language.

PowerShell may not be the best example of porting your pipeline code to another language. For this book we've used Shell scripts running in Linux environments. A more realistic conversion would be to a language that gives you more power than Shell, but is still very Linux friendly. So now, let's look at these scripts written in Python.

Python

Listing 5-5 shows the build stage in Python.

Listing 5-5. Python Build Stage Script

```
application_type = application.type

if application_type == 'java':
    subprocess.run(['mvn', 'clean', 'package'], check=True)
elif application_type == 'netcore':
    subprocess.run(['dotnet', 'restore'], check=True)
```

```
    subprocess.run(['dotnet', 'build', '-c', 'Release'],
    check=True)
elif application_type == 'node':
    subprocess.run(['npm', 'install'], check=True)
else
    raise Exception(f'Unable to build application type
    {application_type}.')
```

Much like the Shell script and the PowerShell script, we simply
determine the application type and perform the standard build commands
for each language. Listing 5-6 illustrates the unit test stage.

Note   This is a slimmed down Python script. It does not include the
shebang or any import statements that would be required. We're focusing
solely on the logic in the script. The version of Python shown here is 3.6.

Listing 5-6. Python Unit Test Stage Script

```
application_type = application.type
test_path = test.path

if application_type == 'java':
    subprocess.run(['mvn', 'test'], check=True)
elif application_type == 'netcore':
    subprocess.run(['dotnet', 'test', test_path], check=True)
elif application_type == 'node':
    subprocess.run(['npm', 'run', 'test'], check=True)
else
    raise Exception(f'Unable to test application type
{application_type}.')
```

By now the beauty and simplicity of the pattern should be taking hold. You've seen Shell, PowerShell, and now Python. Even if you don't regularly use these languages, by sticking with standards and keeping things simple, the code is very easy to read. More importantly, it's very easy to port should that need ever arise. Listing 5-7 shows the archive stage.

Listing 5-7. Python Archive Stage Script

```
registry = archive.registry
namespace = archive.namespace
repository = archive.repository
image = f'{registry}/{namespace}/{repository}:latest'

subprocess.run(['docker', 'login', registry,
    '-u', docker_username, '-p', docker_password], check=True)
subprocess.run(['docker', 'build', '-t', image], check=True)
subprocess.run(['docker', 'push',  image], check=True)
```

Finally, listing 5-8 illustrates the deploy stage.

Listing 5-8. Python Deploy Stage Script

```
registry = archive.registry
namespace = archive.namespace
repository = archive.repository
image = f'{registry}/{namespace}/{repository}:latest'
subprocess.run(['docker', 'run', '-dP', image], check=True)
```

Now imagine your team decides that all this Shell and PowerShell and Python stuff is for the birds; they want to use Golang! Not a problem, you say! At this point it would be a trivial task to research how to issue commands via Golang, and rewrite the pipeline. Of course, this all depends on how complex your pipeline is. However, by sticking to standards and not having a lot of "one-off" code, this task becomes much easier.

Custom Script Hooks

The most important rule of the generic pipeline, without a doubt, is to strictly adhere to standards. Standards are your friends; do not deviate from them. They are the only thing that makes a generic pipeline work, period. Standards keep the playing field level and ensure that all applications are handled in the exact same manner, every time.

This is invaluable when it comes to placing new languages on the pipeline, debugging, as well as adding new features. Without a doubt teams will come to you and ask (or even expect) for one-off changes that may apply only to their application. Do not give in to these requests! It may seem benign at first, and you're happy to oblige. But over time all those tweaks begin to add up. Bugs start to creep in and it becomes increasingly difficult to diagnose and fix issues. The cost and effort required to maintain the overall pipeline skyrockets. And let's not forget, a fix here may break another application over there.

By making all development teams play by the same rules, you ensure everyone gets treated the same and the pipeline remains very stable. You're going to make some people unhappy, and you may be faced with having to turn some teams away. If a team has an application that requires a lot of custom work, you may have to say "sorry, build your own pipeline." This is life with a generic pipeline.

However, being a DevOps team, you don't want to be too rigid. After all, the development teams are your customers. And we want to have happy customers! So what options do we have if want to keep standards in place but also give the teams some flexibility in customizing things. You can offer your teams script hooks.

Script hooks are simply an opportunity for teams to inject their own functionality via scripts into the pipeline. This can be a happy medium in keeping the pipeline clean from a lot of custom logic and allowing your development teams to do custom stuff. Let's look at what script hooks look like and how you can incorporate them into your pipeline.

Pre- and Postpipeline Hooks

Common areas for custom hooks are at the beginning and end of the pipeline. This allows a development team to define custom actions that are to be performed before or after their application is built or deployed. Some common actions may include:

- Installing any custom software, plug-ins, packages, etc. that are required by the application

- Performing any clean-up actions needed by a new version of the application

- Performing any data migrations or clean-up that may be needed

What is nice about these hooks is while they give development teams more flexibility, they're also quite easy for the DevOps team to implement. Providing a hook at the beginning and end of the pipeline is accomplished by simply running a Shell script that is provided by the development team. Figure 5-1 illustrates the flow.

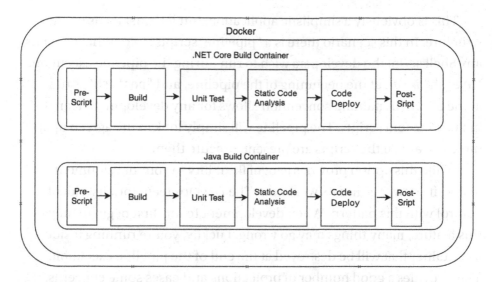

Figure 5-1. *Implementing pre- and post scripts in the pipeline*

As Figure 5-1 shows, we're still running inside a container specific to our language. Nothing has changed in that regard. However, you now are executing custom scripts at the beginning and end of the pipeline. In this scenario the development teams would provide a directory in their code repository containing the scripts. The naming convention of the directory and scripts would be standardized for the pipeline. Imagine a directory structure like the following:

- Code Repo
  - /src
  - /pipeline_scripts
    - pre.sh
    - post.sh
  - /assets
  - /scripts
  - index.html

This is obviously a simplistic application, but let's just focus on the structure. In this scenario there is a "pipeline_scripts" folder that contains any Shell script the developers wish to run during the pipeline execution. "pre.sh" is run at the beginning of the pipeline, and "post.sh" is run at the end. This naming convention allows for any development team to include custom scripts. The pipeline will simply look in the agreed upon directory and, if the scripts are present, execute them.

While this option provides a lot of flexibility to your development teams, its power is also its weakness. The DevOps team forfeits a lot of control with this pattern. When development teams first begin to utilize this feature, many things may go wrong. Luckily, you're running inside a container that will be destroyed at the end of the pipeline execution. This provides a good number of protections and eases some concerns. If a team commits a bad hook script and wrecks the pipeline execution, we can simply throw away the container and try again. This is the beauty of running in a containerized environment. However, there are still a few guidelines that should be followed when implementing pipeline hooks:

- *Run Custom Scripts with Least Privilege*: There will be many stages in the pipeline that require logging into third-party systems or performing actions that require higher access. This is fine if you wrote the code and know what it's doing. It becomes more challenging when you're running custom scripts. Always run custom scripts with a lower level account that has fewer permissions. The last thing you want is a stray script doing horrible things with an administrator account.

- *You Wrote It, You Own It*: When providing this feature to teams, it's extremely important to limit the amount of support your team provides when issues arise from custom scripts. The main reason is you will quickly become a support team for scripts you did not write. You must be firm and inform teams that if they choose to write custom scripts, they must support them. It's your job to provide proper logging so they know what went wrong.

- *Always, Always Run Inside a Container*: These scripts will most likely do things that change the environment, install packages, etc. You want to ensure this happens in a container so it does not affect your platform or other pipeline executions.

- *Trust No One, and Log Everything*: Don't trust that any script is safe. Remember the first point, run with fewer permissions, and log everything the script does!

If that list didn't scare you off, then it's time to talk about taking this pattern one step further with stage hooks.

Stage Hooks

Pre- and postscript hooks provide a great deal of functionality. In fact, it's rare to have this level of control over how the pipeline executes. And even when development teams do have a lot of pipeline control, it's administered via normal work processes. A feature request is raised with the DevOps team who then implements a change. By using stage hooks, this process is turned on its head.

Supporting pre- and post hooks will encourage teams to add more custom functionality at the stage level and less custom functionality in the before and after hooks. Common pre- and posthook actions are similar to before and after hook actions. They typically include:

- Installing additional packages that are needed for build and unit tests

- Using a different unit test framework than what is currently supported by the DevOps team

- Running additional tests, then combining test coverage reports

Just like with the pre- and post scripts, the custom stage scripts get picked up and run before each stage, as shown in Figure 5-2.

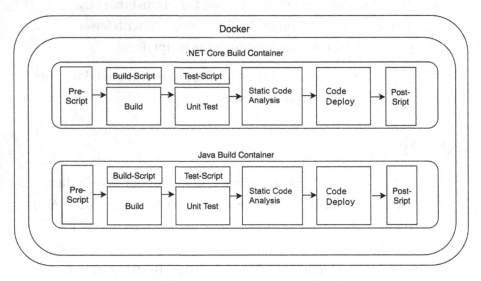

Figure 5-2. *Build and Unit Test custom scripts being injected*

In this scenario, we provide the development teams with a prebuild and preunit test script hook. These would be the most common areas for hooks to be present. For instance, it's unlikely to need any kind of hook for static code analysis, security scans, or deployments. Those are stages that are sacred and should not be altered. Build and Unit Test, however, are areas in which the teams may have legitimate needs for custom functionality. As with pre- and post scripts, standardization is your friend. The application repo may look like the following:

- Code Repo
  - `/src`
  - `/pipeline_scripts`
    - `pre.sh`
    - `post.sh`
    - `pre-build.sh`
    - `pre-test.sh`
  - `/assets`
  - `/scripts`
  - `index.html`

The script naming here is subtle but very important. By prefixing the scripts with "pre" it's an indicator to the development teams that this is a prebuild script only. You still intend to execute your pipeline code, and you should. These are not meant to be full overrides of your pipeline code, although you could certainly do that if you wish. However, it's been our experience that doing that invites a lot of support requests and broken pipeline executions.

Custom script hooks are actually meant to provide the DevOps team with a bit of breathing room. It allows you to give your development teams options for expanding the capabilities of the pipeline to meet their needs, but in a controlled setting. If done properly, you can keep your standards-based pipeline running smoothly while giving your development teams the flexibility to tailor parts of the pipeline to their specific needs.

Where to Go from Here

You've now been introduced to a shared generic pipeline with Docker. You've seen how you can extend its functionality and provide your development teams with all the features they need and then some. So where do you go from here?

Hopefully we've shown you some things that you can practically apply to your own pipelines. Even if you don't go out and refactor your pipelines to be generic across the board, you may have seen some things that can help in your day to day activities. This book was written from practical knowledge from folks who've been down this road. If you decide to embark on the truly generic shared pipeline, remember these tips:

- *Standards, Standards, Standards*: We were absolutely a broken record with this, but it's true. The only way a generic pipeline will succeed is with clearly defined standards and only one way to do things (i.e., build, test, etc.). The more customization you place in the pipeline, the harder it will be to maintain and troubleshoot.

- *Say No, and Often*: Development teams will always ask for more—new features, customization requests, and special exceptions for their team or project. You have to say no more often than you say yes. A generic pipeline is meant for all teams to use, and if that is the case it must be truly generic. Learn to say no; that word is one of your best friends.

- *Over Communicate with Teams*: As you build the pipeline and maintain it, you'll need to make changes from time to time. Some of these are big; some go unnoticed. It's very important to over communicate with your development teams. They are putting a lot of trust in your pipeline and they want to know what's going on. Even if there is a small change, publicize it. Ensure everyone knows what is happening with upcoming changes long before you do them.

Now you're ready to tackle the generic pipeline. By using Docker and strictly adhering to standards, you can deliver a CI/CD experience unlike most others. When done properly, you will not only support your development teams but quite possibly the whole organization. Don't be surprised if teams come knocking at your door to get on board. Embrace the change, and you and your team can deliver great things.

Index

© Brandon Atkinson, Dallas Edwards 2018
B. Atkinson and D. Edwards, *Generic Pipelines Using Docker*,
https://doi.org/10.1007/978-1-4842-3655-0